KT-387-648

just what I've always wanted

THE SECRET FORMULA FOR CHOOSING THE PERFECT GIFT

Attract the object of your desire with a flower sculpture - in the form of a magnet.

just what I've always wanted

THE SECRET FORMULA FOR CHOOSING THE PERFECT GIFT

SUSANNAH CONSTANTINE & PIA MAROCCO
RESEARCH AND ADDITIONAL TEXT BY GEORGINA GOODMAN
FOREWORD BY SHIRLEY CONRAN

QUADRILLE

Thanks to all our friends who so generously shared their ideas with us, especially Helen.
SUSANNAH & PIA

First published in 1995 by
Quadrille Publishing Limited
9 Irving Street, London WC2H 7AT

Design: Michael, Harriet & David at johnson banks
Consultant: Sarah Temple
Photography: Martin Barraud
Styling: Tanya Haughton & Rebecca Alleway
Modelmaker: Mallard Models
Additional research: Stephanie Crean

British Library Cataloguing-in-Publication Data
A catalogue record for this book is available from the British Library.

ISBN 1 899988 35 1

Printed in Hong Kong
Produced by Mandarin Offset Ltd

contents

foreword

Like many people, I love giving presents; however, as everyone in this world gets busier if they have a job, and shorter of money if they haven't, sometimes the pain of worrying what to give can almost outweigh the pleasure of giving.

Many a stout heart sinks at the sight of a lengthening Christmas gift list, thinking of the worry, time and effort it will involve, as well as an expenditure that might well solve some third world country's balance of payment problem.

In my family, we have a money limit on Christmas gifts, which sometimes leads to argument. ("How could you possibly have bought mum a Penny Black for under ten quid?")

Some of the nicest gifts cost nothing. One of the most thoughtful and loving gifts I ever received was from my mother-in-law-to-be, who gave me for Christmas a collection of photographs of my bridegroom as a little boy.

It's only the thought that counts if there has been some thought, which doesn't always include that involved in recycling gifts from other people. But be careful that your thought suits the recipient, not yourself. My eight-year-old son once proudly handed me on my birthday a cigar box into which was jammed a dead, flea-riddled rat. He clearly thought that I'd adore it as much as he did. ("But you loved the fossilized stoat's head I gave you last Christmas…")

This same son, when twelve years old, was handy with a toolbox; tired of being expected to do all the nasty little jobs that I couldn't, he gave me a birthday gift of six pink cards marked 'IOU One Nasty Job'; he is now 39 and I still have three of them; as I saved these up for really desperate occasions, I quickly found that I was less helpless than I thought.

When giving to that difficult group, the rich, you'll be delighted to hear that with them it really is the thought that counts: the nice ones are embarrassed if they think you've felt obliged to spend more than you can afford. The rich love personalized presents, with their initials or name on them - handkerchiefs, matches, postcards and pencils always seem welcome.

If you particularly want to give a lavish present to someone, don't give it at Christmas; the recipient may gaze at it with a sinking heart and feel guilty because he or she hasn't given you a gift of similar value. I often send such gifts, or special cards, drawings or poems on Valentine's Day, which seems an appropriate time to let someone know that you're fond of them.

As eveyone thinks that their own taste is immaculate, when giving something personal, such as a picture or a sweater, I always give a let-out to the recipient, saying "If it isn't to your taste, please exchange it, or tell me what you'd rather have." I am particularly careful to say this to my daughter-in-law.

So that I'm never caught short of a gift when I haven't time to shop (a chronic condition of the working mother) I keep a permanent gift drawer for little gifts that I buy when I see them; also in this drawer is a gift-wrapping box in which are scissors, a Sellotape dispenser, white tissue and cream, narrow real satin baby ribbon; you might try this with a more daring colour scheme.

I love giving books, partly because they're an easy shape to wrap and send by post. And if you can't decide what book to send… clearly this book has been written with love and thought and care: so it seems to me to be… the perfect gift.

Shirley Conran

the secret formula

In Oscar Wilde's "The Nightingale and the Rose", a nightingale gives up her life so that a student can give the gift of a red rose to the girl he loves. The rose fails to impress the girl and the nightingale has died in vain. Why didn't the student know that the red rose was the wrong gift? How could he have chosen exactly the right one?
At some point we have all been in a similar situation and got it horribly wrong. The anxiety of slipping up provokes questions in the back of our minds: "Will they like it?", "Is it what they want?" We have even cunningly developed phrases and expressions in a bid to pre-empt the embarrassment of making a blunder. "If you don't like it, you can exchange it" and "Oh, it is just something silly" are two examples of the way we demonstrate how insecure we are about choosing something appropriate.
So, where is the answer? How can we be sure to pick the perfect present? Could there be a formula for getting it right? Yes, there is and this is it.

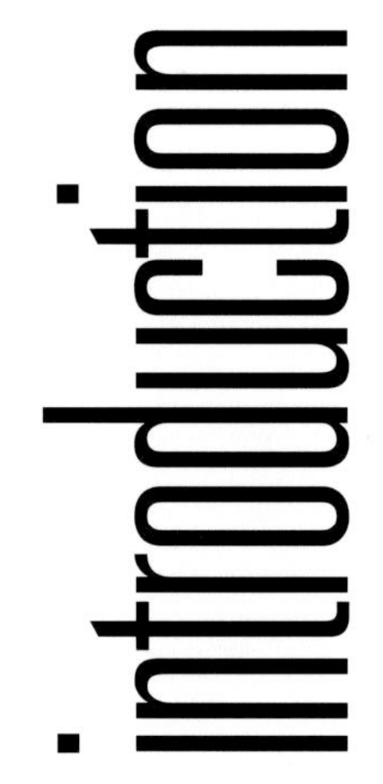

The answer lies not in the gift itself, but in the person you are giving to and the relationship you have with them. We all make the mistake of thinking that all gifts mean the same thing to all people. Wrong. A bunch of red roses sent to your lover represents something entirely different from a bunch of flowers sent to your boss. The bunch of flowers hasn't changed, the receiver has.

In order to find the right gift we have to pay attention to the recipient and his psychological make-up. The key to this is to understand his motivations and tune into what makes him tick. Knowing what *drives* a person is the most effective way to understanding their likes and dislikes. In order to make this task simple, we have to be able to slot people into categories.

You might think that categorising people is very difficult or even impossible, unless you know them inside out; for our purposes however, it is surprisingly straightforward.

We can use a method developed in behavioural psychology which categorises the main motivations into three groups:
Affiliation. Achievement. Power.

Those in the Affiliation group want to please and make friends. They need constant affirmation that they are loved and that they belong. Those in the Achievement group are driven by a desire to succeed and prove themselves. Their ambition is to be respected and recognised for their achievements. The Power group wants to be in control and influence its environment. They are confident and forceful.

Each group looks at gifts in varying ways and takes different meanings from them.

Each and every one of us is a member of one of these groups, and although we might bridge two of them, we never belong to all three.

Opposite is a chart which will help you choose which type of person you are giving to. If you can pick the right group, you will select the right present - the Secret Formula is as easy as that.

Throughout the book you will find each of the ideas annotated with one or more of the three symbols shown opposite as an aid to deciding whether the suggested gift would be suitable.

AFFILIATION people look at the method of presentation, more than the gift itself.
These people are more concerned with the effort that has gone into the wrapping and the choice of paper.
In fact, the value of the actual gift is of minimal importance, as the act of receiving is the assurance they are looking for.

ACHIEVEMENT people see gifts as trophies or tokens. Tokens that reveal the high esteem you hold them in.
They will interpret the value or challenge of the gift as how much you appreciate them and gifts are well received that demonstrate this fact.
For them the best wrapping paper still has the label of the shop on it.

POWER people actually prefer giving to receiving, but they do like presents that are useful to them. Don't waste your time with elaborate wrapping and don't be too disappointed if a letter of thanks never even materialises. Detail is irrelevant to them. If the present helps them in their quest for control, it will be much appreciated.

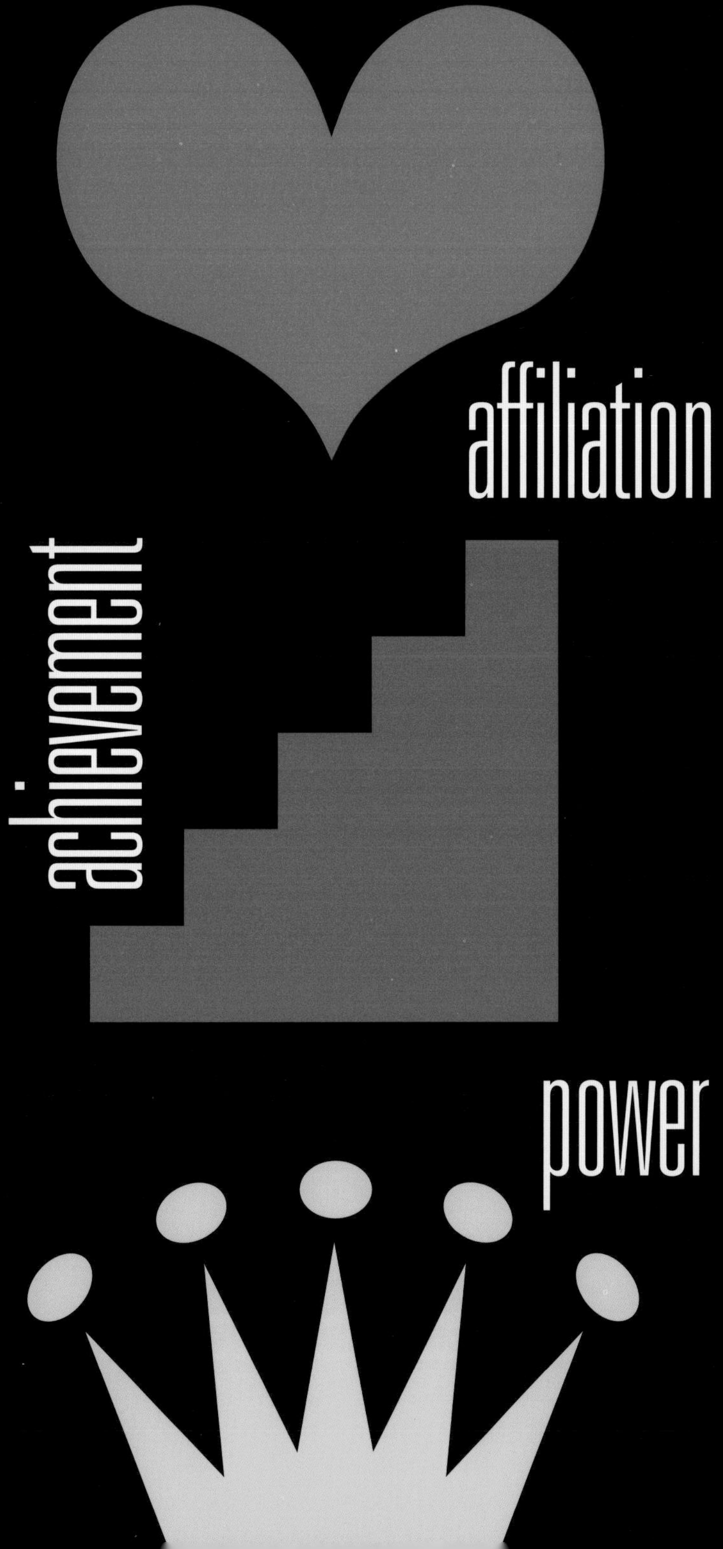

affiliation

achievement

power

Affiliation
needs to be liked
wants to please
friendly
caring
sympathetic
likes to join in
indecisive
doesn't make waves
needs to belong
wants approval
looks after friends
sociable
insecure

Achievement
active
determined
ambitious
competitive
works hard
winner mentality
likes flattery
self-conscious
confident
wants to have the best
wants respect

Power
intelligent
dominant
decisive
leaders
arrogant
confident
unemotional
money driven
forceful
influential

They fell in love and lived happily ever after...
Falling is the easy part - take a man and a woman, add a sprinkling of love dust, and bingo! They have fallen in love. Maintaining and improving that initial blinding feeling is quite another fairytale, however. A budding romance can evolve into a lasting union, but to do so it needs continual care and attention and here, as is so often the case, actions speak louder than words. It is the thoughtful gestures, the special efforts and the little tokens that are essential to keep love flowering.

This includes practicalities, such as doing your fair share of the domestic chores, but it also means taking time out from the daily routine to think 'gifts'.

Dump domesticity and come home with an unexpected bunch of flowers, present a peace offering after a tumultuous skirmish or simply leave a love note on the pillow. It's easy, effective and, most importantly, fun.

lovers

getting noticed

GIRL *meets boy, boy fancies girl - what next? Taking the initial meeting a stage further can be heart-stopping. However, it only takes a little ingenuity to make this dilemma less palpitating and achieve the success you desire.*

• **GETTING noticed by *Imran Khan*, the world-famous cricketer, a man who is, let's face it, spoilt for choice, is a challenge of gargantuan proportions. One smitten female, wanting to get his attention, sent him a vast box of Belgian chocolates.** "So what?", you cry. Ah, but she was smart: included in the cholesterol-ridden feast was a cricket ball wrapped up in a note that declared, "The ball is in your court". He was bowled over.❤

IT'S TIME to take the plunge and contact that gorgeous individual you met at a friend's wedding. If the thought of picking up the phone is too earth-shattering, then send something instead. A pair of **hiking boots** and an invitation to set off for the hills may seem somewhat eccentric, but a positive reply would mean a whole day alone together and the possibility of a romantic evening meal when you return home, famished after all that fresh air and exercise.

EVE tempted Adam with **an apple** and the rest is history. Send your would-be mate an apple with a note saying "Try me" and your phone number, surely a challenge no red-blooded male could refuse.❤

IF YOU want to be a little more romantic, try taking out **a classified ad** in the lonely hearts section of a newspaper, then deliver the paper to your love, having encircled your advert with a heart. Alternatively, ring-and-run after fixing **a heart-shaped wreath** of flowers on their front door, or track down their car and secretly leave **a lone rose**, with your telephone number attached, on the windscreen.❤

SPECIAL DAYS offer the ideal excuse to make a move upon the one you admire. Valentine's Day is such an opportunity. It is the perfect chance for you to use cloak-and-dagger methods to reveal your romantic objectives. Rather than just the one bunch of red roses, throw caution to the winds, break into your piggy bank and arrange for the delivery of twelve red roses, every hour, for twelve hours. Keep them in suspense and only send your name with the last bunch.

heart stopping.

Equally as good are birthdays and anniversaries. Charm your intended by finding out that special date and at dawn on the day, arrive on the doorstep, **champagne breakfast** in hand, along with **newspapers** and **flowers.**

Sometimes romances need a little extra push to get them started. You've been making eyes at the same person for months, but your glances have gone unheeded. Go to a pharmacy and purchase a pair of **off-the-peg spectacles**. Take them to the next social occasion and when you spot your prey, simply stroll up and hand over the eye wear. Put on your cheekiest grin and say, "I think you need these as you obviously haven't been able to see me", then walk coolly away. Within seconds you will be the focus of attention.

• As the prelude to romance, a well-known Italian playboy asked the beautiful American socialite *Cosima von Bulow* out for a cup of coffee. So innocent was his request that she accepted. Upon leaving her house to meet him, she was greeted by a delivery man armed with a brand new espresso machine, two cups, freshly ground coffee and a bottle of milk. Moments later the Italian swept through her door, bearing a bowl of sugar and declaring, "This is the essential ingredient to the perfect espresso". Five cups of coffee and two hours later, Cosima had been won over by his charms and willingly agreed to have dinner with him that night.

Flowers for getting noticed

Acacia - Concealed love
Almond Blossom - Hope
Damask Rose - Bashful love
Enchanter's Nightshade - Fascination, sorcery
Fuchsia - Confiding love
Lilac - First emotions of love
Peach Blossom - I am your captive
Red Tulip - Declaration of love
Rose Geranium - Preference

I II III

Arrange for the delivery of twelve roses, every hour, for twelve hours.

i love you

THERE *are occasions when you simply want to say "I love you". Be it with a gesture or a gift, act on that impulse to shout your devotion from the highest building, but use the element of surprise to make more of an impact.*

IF YOU love someone as much as all the stars in the sky, search out **a stunning glass bottle** (antique or modern) and fill it with gold and silver confetti stars.

PERHAPS your style and sentiments are more down to earth and the amount of love you feel is equivalent to all the pebbles on the beach. A **ceramic bowl** (a handmade piece or a simple coloured one) containing a selection of beautiful stones represents a personal message – the expense can be tailored to suit your resources and the occasion for the gift.

THE financier ***Ivan Boesky*** gave his girlfriend **a piano** with a card reading "You are the music of my life". A **harmonica**, a **tape** or **tickets to a concert** would be less extravagant alternatives on this theme.

CONSIDER yourself a bit of a movie star? Love your darling to distraction? Then show your love by writing him a love letter accompanied by a set of Polaroids of yourself in various poses visualising your true feelings. This unique Polaroid love story will not only be adored by its recipient, but also be huge fun to make.

sweet nothings:

ARE YOU in the habit of whispering sweet nothings for hours whilst smothering your sweetheart's face with butterfly kisses? If so, you will need a rather more dramatic gesture to demonstrate your undying love effectively. Think bold, think big, in fact think **carpet of flowers on the bedroom floor**!

darling:

• WHEN *Steve McQueen* fell head over heels in love with *Ali McGraw*, he sent her a bunch of his favourite flowers, white daisies. Driving by her house in the evening, he was surprised to see his gift unceromoniously dumped in her dustbin. Not taken aback in the slightest by her rebuff, he planted his next bunch in a shiny new trash can. This time she returned the lot and the to-ing and fro-ing continued until she fell for his irresistible charm and wit.

sorry

All quarrels *and arguments are horrible at the best of times, but rows between lovers are the most dreadful. Inevitably they result in one partner storming out, leaving the other feeling utterly wretched and alone.*

Your fine china is in smithereens on the kitchen floor and your relationship is in as many pieces, it's going to take a bold move to patch up this one. If you're the one who has left in a rage and you both need time to forgive and forget, try **fluttering a lone rose petal** through the letter box every day for ten days. On the eleventh day, post the naked stem with a note saying "This is how I feel without you" and, hopefully, all will be forgiven.❤

make up

Saying that little word 'sorry' and meaning it can seem as difficult as dragging an elephant uphill. However, if sorry you are, **sorry you must say**, so get over the difficulty by saying it in an unusual way. Why not say it in a different language?

A couple had a classic dispute over a razor. She had used it to shave her legs and he reacted as though it had been used to mow the lawn. Unable to pacify her angry man, she bought **a rubber duck** of the bath variety, painted it white and skewered an olive branch through its beak. Crouching outside, she tapped on the kitchen window and 'flew' the makeshift dove of peace past the pane. Thankfully, he rediscovered his sense of humour and the dispute was over.❤

If you've fought and the emotional wounds have left you weak and beaten, buy or make **a white flag** and surrender to the enemy. If all goes well, they will lay down their weapons and sweep you into a passionate embrace of forgiveness.❤

You've said something you regret but his pride is wounded and he will not listen to your apologies. Buy him a **peace pipe** symbolizing a war-free zone. He is sure to give in.❤

If after a tiff, your sulky partner refuses to speak to you, send her a **powder compact** with **"Let's make up" written in lipstick** on the mirror. Short, sweet and simple, but very effective.❤

forgive

top ten gifts

In general, men have much larger egos than women and what they want are things that they can show off; in short, items that say, "I'm a man". Even though it might be his top choice, few of us can afford the first gift on the list, so give him a model of his favourite machine instead.

Contrary to popular male belief, women do not like receiving blatantly sexy underwear or domestic appliances; the former make her feel cheap, the latter make her feel dowdy. A woman wants to feel feminine and beautiful, independent but at the same time protected and any gift that matches this description will be ideal. It is a wise girl who lets her man choose the more expensive items.

Girls to Boys

1 - Fast car or motorbike.
2 - Hi-fi equipment or a personal stereo.❤
3 - Weight-training equipment.
4 - Leather jacket (there's a Marlon Brando lurking in every man).
5 - Wallet (to show off his credit cards).
6 - A subscription to the sports channel/sporting tickets.❤
7 - Infra-red binoculars (very James Bond).
8 - Penknife (the bigger, the better).
9 - A customized steering wheel or gear stick.
10 - A personal organizer or mobile phone.

Boys to Girls

1 - Diamonds (from a tiny chip to a huge rock) are a girl's best friend.❤
2 - Cashmere or silk (anything).
3 - A weekend/holiday in a romantic setting.❤
4 - A watch.
5 - Shoes (but not the sensible variety).
6 - Hand or travel bags.
7 - Chocolates (of course).❤
8 - Flowers (a hand-picked bunch, or a lovingly-chosen bouquet with special meaning.❤
9 - A specially inscribed poem (either written or chosen by you).❤
10 - A day in the gym or beauty clinic (especially after all those chocolates).

with all my heart

A candlelit dinner is the ultimate romantic occasion, but often takes place amongst impersonal surroundings in a restaurant. To make this dinner really special and to show that you've thought about it in advance, why not have a discreet word with the restaurant prior to your date, requesting that a special dish be added to the dessert menu just for you. For example: '**Apple of my eye pie**, served with lashings of love from...(your name)'.❤

• Throughout his enduringly happy marriage to actress *Nanette Newman*, film maker *Bryan Forbes* has often sent her heart-shaped objects from his travels around the world. Engraved on each gift is a declaration of love and the name of the location. The result is a growing collection of heart-shaped items with "I love you in Paris" or "I love you in New York/ Rome/Timbuktu" depending where he was at the time.❤

Any gift to a loved one made in or bearing the shape of a heart will be a sure winner, whether for Valentine's Day or just the fancy takes you. Here are some suggestions:❤
Flower sculpture
Cushion (with embroidered message)
Box of chocolates
Photo frame
China box
Locket containing photo, lock of hair or message
Stone/Leaf (found objects)
Cut gems
Candlesticks
Soap

tiny
If you have **a pet name for your lover** why not adopt its namesake at your local zoo or wildlife park.

long distance love

Conducting *a love affair long distance is something most people have to cope with at some point. Experience in making international telephone calls, proficiency in sticking the correct stamps on airmail letters and fluency in airport check-in desk conversation are just a few of the skills needed to maintain an overseas relationship. Sometimes a little initiative is needed to keep things going.*

love letters

LOVE LETTERS, though always treasured, are especially appreciated when circumstances have forced a couple apart. Bring this time-honoured romantic tradition up-to-date with the wonders of modern technology by recording your passionate feelings onto a **cassette tape**. Not only will your sweetheart be privy to your thoughts, but they will be able to listen to your dulcet tones whenever they wish. ❤

DURING the separation make sure you have the means to stay in touch. Buy **a stamp for each day** that you are apart, slip them into a **silken pouch** and produce them as a farewell love token, to ensure that out of sight is not out of mind. ❤

THE TELEPHONE is essential for conducting an affair over a vast distance, but business travellers don't always have access to a free one. Make your midnight caller a parting gift of a fistful of **phone cards** to keep the lines of communication open.

YOU ARE going away, leaving your dearest heartbroken and lonely. Make the time apart easier by arranging a **standing order of flowers** on a daily/ weekly/monthly basis to keep your lover's heart from aching. ❤

PERHAPS even more than the spoken word, music is a wonderfully evocative way to open the floodgates of memory. Many a parted lover has shed a tear when hearing that special song on the radio that they have danced or made love to. Compile a **cassette tape** with **all the songs you both love** so your partner can bring you closer at any time of the day or night. ❤

REMIND your lover of you every moment of the day with a **pendant** or locket to hang around their neck. Have your name engraved on one side and, on the other, **"Good Morning, Good Night, God Bless"**. Tell them, "Good Morning is the first thing you say at the start of a new day, Good Night is the last and God Bless you always". Your thoughts and prayers will thus be close to their heart at all times. ❤

Before you leave town for a business trip or holiday, ***fill the fridge*** *with edible delicacies to encourage your partner to stay home... alone.*

HELP COUNT the days till you will be together again: buy a **diary** for your soon-to-be-lovesick amour and write a sentimental message on each of the days that you will be apart. If the separation will amount to months, **customize a glossy landscape calendar** by sticking cut-out pictures of yourself on every photograph - dancing in the daffodils, kissing in the cornfields and scaling the ski slopes.

IN THE event of having to leave a helpless, hopeless partner in the jungle of domesticity, **fill the fridge** with edible delicacies to keep the wolf from the door and encourage them to stay home… alone.

Long-distance flowers of love

Fir - Time
Heliotrope - Devotion
Iris - Message
Myrtle - Love in absence
Nutmeg Geranium - I shall meet you
Pansy - Think of me
Rosemary - Rememberance
Star of Bethlehem - The light of your path
Sweet Pea - Departure
Thistle - I'll never forget thee
White Periwinkle - Sweet remembrances
Zinnia - Absence

aphrodisiacs

THE WAY *to a man's heart, so they say, is through his stomach; for girls, a man who can cook or at least shows willing in the kitchen is an irresistible potential partner. Food has been used to entice, bewitch and capture the hearts of the opposite sex for centuries. Whether it's intended to woo a potential partner or to rekindle a dying flame, this lovingly prepared meal with its combination of aphrodisiac ingredients shouldn't fail. Set the mood with candles, fill the air with erotic aromas and slip into something suitably slinky. Upon the arrival of your dinner guest present a hand-scripted menu as follows:*

Welcome To Cupid's Kitchen

STARTER
Wild Mushroom and Herb Tart

MAIN COURSE
Free Range Breast of Chicken,
Marinated in Ginger and Saffron
Stuffed with Pine Nuts and Garlic
Served with
Baby Parsnips Glazed with Honey
A Warm Salad of Wild Lettuce
dressed with Truffle Oil

DESSERT
Lime and Pomegranate Mousse
With an Apricot Coulis
Followed by Coffee and Chocolates

with love xxx

Freeze the ring in an ice-cube and pop it in her favourite drink.

the proposal

MARRIAGE *is the supreme commitment to enduring love and, for the most part, it is the actual proposal and the occasion on which it was made that remains engraved in the memories of the two people concerned. The immortal words "Will you marry me?" are for many women recorded in expectant minds from a very early age. The fertile female imagination develops an image of her intended materializing on the back of a rearing white stallion or swinging athletically from a helicopter into her moonlit bedroom with a ring nestling in a box of chocolates. Realistically, whatever the circumstances, nothing can take away the magic of those four words. However, as a proposal is intended to be a-once-in-a-lifetime question, why not make it an event worth remembering.*

ASKING the girl of your dreams to become your wife, be the mother of your children and spend the rest of her life within the security of your protective arms is an occasion of importance. The great moment can be further enhanced by disguising your intentions until the last minute. A simple walk in the countryside can become as heavenly as a stroll through the Garden of Eden if you propose, and are accepted, somewhere along the way. However, it will be even more in keeping with paradise if along the route you have previously **hidden a bottle of champagne, two glasses and her ring** in the secret nook of a tree or under a moss-covered rock. Imagine her surprise when you offer her a glass of champagne in the middle of nowhere, followed by her cries of amazement when she discovers the ring.

ONE SURE way to hit the spot would be to buy **a Jack-in-the-Box** and fix the ring to the puppet's hand. Watch her jump - for joy - when she opens the package.

will you...

ANOTHER cool way to pop the question is to **freeze the engagement ring in an ice-cube** and drop it into a glass of her favourite tipple, or **place it in an oyster** before sharing the delights of a shellfish and candlelit champagne dinner.

A SIMPLE way of making sure that your bride-to-be can treasure your proposal for ever is to **engrave it on a crystal or silver cup** and present it to her. She can then return the gesture by engraving "Yes, I will!"

Flowers for a proposal of marriage

Fern - Sincerity
Iris - A message for you
Linden Tree (Lime) - Matrimony
Everlasting Pea - Will you go with me?
Rose Petals: Red - Yes; White - No
Striped Pink - Refusal

ARE YOU one of those rare men who can count patience amongst their list of virtues? And do you have a tinge of green in your fingertips? If so, then this proposal idea could be for you, as it requires forward planning and a basic knowledge of gardening. **Plant flowering bulbs** or even **mustard and cress in the shape of the phrase "Will you marry me?"** and when in full bloom show or give your prospective bride the arrangement. After you've taken so much trouble, how could the answer be anything but "Yes"?

IT WAS their fifth Christmas together and once again the ever-hopeful girl prayed for that simple ring representing a lasting commitment. Come Christmas morning, she was devastated to discover **a box of vast proportions** from her beau. Inside was a birdcage. Momentarily blinded by disappointed tears, she noticed neither the little stuffed bird nor its precious offering. For there, clasped in its beak, was her future husband's handwritten proposal encircled by the ring he had chosen for her.

WHICHEVER of these ways you choose, your beloved will be totally entranced by your originality and sheer thoughtfulness and, at the same time, she'll realize that life with you certainly won't be dull and boring!

...marry me?

anniversary

A WEDDING *anniversary is an occasion which gives us the scope to be as romantic as we wish. Unlike birthdays or Christmas, it is a celebration of equal significance for both people. The commemoration of the day that began your life together is sadly often forgotten. However, it is worth remembering that anniversary gifts are a unique and intimate recommitment to your status as man and wife.*

• *Calvin Klein's* bestselling perfume, Eternity, was born out of a very special anniversary gift that he gave to his beautiful wife, *Kelly.* At auction he bought the eternity ring given to *Wallis Simpson* by the *Duke of Windsor*, a symbol of the great love which toppled him from the throne of England. It seemed appropriate to create a perfume which would capture the magic of this unique and historic piece of jewellry and enable its romantic spirit to be shared by millions.❤

THE DATE of your wedding anniversary is looming. As a welcome change from the obvious bunch of flowers, make up **a model in the shape of the number of years** you have been together.

1 - Cotton
2 - Paper
3 - Leather
4 - Silk
5 - Wood
10 - Tin
15 - Crystal
20 - China
25 - Silver
30 - Pearl
35 - Coral

Do you remember your first meeting, when your heart hit the floor and your stomach fluttered in excited anticipation of a new love affair? If so, a wonderfully romantic idea for an anniversary is to **take your husband or wife back** to that place and make it the focal point for a special day out or a magical night together.❤

THE TREE is the symbol of life. The seeds need to be sown, nurtured and protected, so that it may blossom and grow, like true love. **Planting a tree** together in expectation of watching it mature with the years is another confirmation of your commitment to an enduring love.❤

FOR ANY anniversary, be it your first, tenth or twentieth, give an equivalent number of items to represent your years spent together. This could be **one bottle of perfume, a course of ten lessons** (flying/golf/ music) or **a twenty-day holiday.** ❤

IF YOU feel like doing something different this time around, pick **a favourite song** which evokes special memories for both of you and **transform it into a special gift.** For example, if Paul Simon's *Diamonds on the Soles of her Shoes* is a her favourite, buy a diamanté bracelet or necklace and present it in a pair of beautiful evening shoes. For the song *Red, Red Wine*, have a bottle of special red wine bearing a specially made label inscribed with the lyrics of this nostalgic song.❤

YOUR WEDDING day may have been years ago, but **the vows you exchanged** stand by you throughout your marriage. A moving gesture would be to reiterate the promises made in the eyes of God by repeating them either in the church where you were married or, if that is geographically impossible, in a favourite place or in your own home.❤

Anniversary flowers
Bluebell - Constancy
Dogwood - Durability
Heliotrope - Devotion
Lilac - Memory
Phlox - We are united
Pink, Double, Red - Pure and ardent love
Pink, Single - Pure love
Strawberry - Esteem and love
White Camellia - Perfect loveliness

...remember?

As a change from the usual bunch of flowers, make up a model in the shape of the number of years you have been together.

search for the locket at the bottom of a goldfish bowl

birthdays & Christmas

THE FIRST *Christmas spent together as a couple is probably the most exciting since your discovery that Father Christmas was, in fact, your festively inebriated father or uncle. Married or not, both birthdays and Christmas are occasions made all the more memorable when spent in the company of the one you love.*

CLASSIC pieces of jewellry such as a pair of earrings, a brooch or a locket are always welcome, but can appear uninspired as gifts. You can enhance their sentimental value with **original presentation** ideas.Why not clip a pair of earrings on a favourite teddy bear, pin a brooch to an apron or dressing gown, or have her search for the locket at the bottom of a goldfish bowl.❤

THIS is the time for our old favourite, **the bunch of roses.** Exquisite though they are, you might be able to make the gift that much more personal by choosing a variety of rose with the **same name as the recipient**. (Hint: ask your local florist to order in the appropriate blooms.)❤

IT IS YOUR partner's twenty-fifth birthday – not a real milestone, but you want to give them a symbolic gift that is truly indicative of your feelings for them. Sit down and think of **twenty five reasons why you love them.** These attributes can be written on paper and framed, carved in wood or engraved on a silver or glass ornament. Though a simple idea, with care and presentation it will mean much more.❤

• **HAVING already given him seven children, authoress *Danielle Steel* decided on a pet as a birthday present for her husband. Not content with the normal variety of domesticated animal, she nevertheless wanted one that was easily housetrained and good with children, so *Coco,* the Vietnamese pot-bellied pig, became the newest addition to their large household.** ❤

CHRISTMAS 'goodwill to all men' does not always reach the kitchen, as the cook in the house is traditionally chained to the kitchen on Christmas morning while the rest of the household relax and enjoy their presents. A luxury Christmas offering to the chef in your home must surely be the services of **a professional cook** who will not only prepare and serve, but also wash up and clear away the debris after the feast.❤

FOR MANY, the pressure from family and friends as to where they'll be spending Christmas and who'll be providing the expected feast is too much to bear and by November they've had enough. In that case **a holiday for two** on a far-off Caribbean island or a romantic city such as Venice or Paris would be the perfect xmas gift: total pampering and no relatives! ❤

WHOSE turn is it to decorate the Christmas tree this year? In theory it's a job to be enjoyed by all the family, but in reality it is usually your other half that ends up doing it at the same time as trying to wrap presents and write cards. Lighten their load by arranging to have a **ready-decorated tree** delivered.❤

enjoy

THE **power of anticlimax** works wonders at Christmas time. Wrap up a sock and place it under the tree. Come Christmas morning, watch your partner bravely try to summon up a smile and splutter out a "Thank you" whilst you in your wisdom know that inside the pathetic offering is a note saying "My other half is under the bed". Inside the sister sock will be all the goodies they had hoped for.❤

Some of the most important relationships we forge in our lives are lasting friendships. The bonds you form with a close friend are unconditional and hold through thick and thin. When all the rest of the world seems to be against you - families, partners or colleagues - it is to your friends that you turn for support; when something wonderful or exciting happens in your life the first person you want to share it with is your best friend, so they can be a part of your happiness.

A close friendship resembles a romantic attachment without any of the emotional ups and downs, the fits of jealousy or the domestic tantrums. It is akin to a relationship with siblings without the rivalry, with parents without the pressure.

A world without friends would be a miserable place, so look after them, treat them with respect and your own life will be all the richer as a result.

tokens of
friendship

thankyou

"WHAT *do you say?" is a familiar question posed to us as children, to which we learn parrot fashion the reply "Thank you". Eventually, we gather the significance of these words and the importance of using them. Throughout our lives our friends are the main focus of our gratitude and a kind act, loving gesture or selfless deed should by rights receive a substantial thank you!*

WE ALL idolise chocolate. Pay homage at its shrine and send a **message of thanks** made up of **chocolate letters.** (Hint: most good confectioners carry individual chocolate letters. If not, make letter-shaped chocolate chip cookies.) ❤

THESE FRIENDS of yours are constantly entertaining. You have been to dinner and spent the weekend with them on countless occasions. You have sponged off them enough times now to warrant the offering of a small gift. For such great entertainers, what about a **dinner party book.** Akin to a visitors book, they can record within it details of every occasion - who sat next to whom as well as what they ate and drank, plus comments from the guests on the evening's entertainment. Amusing to look back on as well as quite useful (it'll stop you serving up that same old chicken dish the Smiths have had three times before).

• WHEN *San Lorenzo*, the famous London restaurant, celebrated its 25th anniversary the owners, Mara and Lorenzo Berni, invited their friends to join them for an evening of food, wine and a good time. As a surprise, all the guests arrived wearing specially made T-shirts printed with a thank-you message and a photograph of the couple inside a heart. The ever-generous duo, who had given twenty-five years of fun to so many, were moved to tears. ❤

THERE ARE certain dinner parties that require more than just a phone call or a thank-you note for the chef's sheer culinary excellence. If you have been lovingly served a three-course Italian meal starting with homemade pasta and the whole evening was 'Bella, bella, magnifico!' then keep to the Continental theme and send something Italian. Some item of **stylish Italian kitchenware** such as an espresso or capuccino maker would be in order for a really special occasion, but a gesture could be a bottle of superb **first-pressed olive oil**, some genuine **20-year old balsamic vinegar** or perhaps a **CD** of some fabulous **Italian opera.** The same idea can be used after a French, Indian, Thai or Chinese dinner. ❤ ♛

CHOOSING the appropriate paper on which to write your thank-you letter can sometimes be as difficult a choice as a gift. Plain white - too starchy, floral notelet - too mumsie. Basically, you want something that has your personality stamped on it, coupled with a relevant visual message to the person you are thanking. Are you asking the impossible? No. The answer lies in the packet of well-thumbed photos from the evening, weekend or holiday spent together. Pick out the best of the bunch and arrange on a photocopier to the desired size, then press the button and, hey presto! **personalised,** original **writing paper.** ❤

CHILDREN understand the art of giving in a far more instinctive and enthusiastic way than adults. Consumer madness hits us all around the age of eight years old, but before this time a found object lovingly presented is, in the eyes of a child, a gift full of wonder and magic. For an adult friend, too, a found object which brings back some mutual memory can be a gift worth more than its weight in gold. A beautiful feather or a wild flower found on a walk with friends could be made into **a paperweight**, a branch from a tree made into **a walking stick.** ❤ ♛

Convey your message of thanks in an individual way by having an item specially made.

A found object which brings back some mutual memory can be a gift worth more than its weight in gold.

Have a beautiful feather, pebble or wildflower found on a walk with friends made into a paperweight.

cheer up

They say that laughter is the best medicine, so waste no time in racing down to the nearest video store to rent or buy a **classic selection of comedy films** or to your book store for **the latest joke book**. Monitor their listening too: for instance, if your friend is forever playing Buddy Guy's album *Damn Right, I've Got The Blues*, swiftly swap it for some **uplifting gospel music** or a foot-tapping **dance album.**

A **bunch of flowers to cheer you up**

Allspice - Compassion
Almond Blossom - Hope
Angelica - Inspiration
Chrysanthemum - Cheerfulness
Fennel - Strength
Golden Rod - Careful encouragement
Iris - A message for you
Lily of the valley - Return of happiness

There will come a time (if it hasn't already arrived) when a friend will do something beyond the call of devoted duty on your behalf. This may be in the form of enduring perpetual tearful midnight calls after a romantic split, looking after your kids or dog whilst you enjoy a week of sun-soaked relaxation, or simply being there in a time of crisis. Either way, give them a reward by presenting them with **a medal to 'The best friend in the world'**. This could be handmade in the form of a badge or embossed in metal, in true Olympian fashion.

We've all *done it: picked up the phone and said a cheerful "Hello", to be greeted by sobs, snufflings and nose blowing. "It's me. I thought nothing could get any worse: my sister is getting married and now I'm ill as well". Yes, it's that miserable species - The Deeply Depressed Friend. Short of a witty card, the customary bunch of flowers and abundant cheery phone calls, there's not much you can do for an ailing friend - or is there? Cheer them up by sending presents to show you are thinking about them and that they have friends who care.*

For any occasion, be it a birthday, Christmas, anniversary or simply to cheer them up on a gloomy Monday, pump up a **bumper load of balloons through your friend's letter box** and relish their astonishment when they return home to find their home filled with festive coloured spheres! (Hint: to blow them up, use a bicycle pump and be sure to knot the ends before releasing them.)

smile

Orange Tree - Generosity
Peppermint - Warmth of feeling

Tease them out of their misery with an **instant beach holiday** - a box filled with **beautiful shells and starfish.** If you can't send them to an island in the sun then bring the beach to them.

Pump up a ***bumper load of balloons through your friend's letter box*** *and relish their astonishment when they return home.*

get well

Whether *the patient is confined to bed suffering from a contagious disease, or just has a touch of the sniffles, it's time to brush up on your bedside manner and administer a dose of gift-giving medicine.*

Eating in bed is always a hazardous operation. Make the invalid's life easier with one of those special **bed trays** with legs, complete with pretty **china.**

Sometimes a really vicious bout of flu will render a friend completely helpless. This is the time to brave the risk of infection, slip into an apron and rustle up some comforting and strength-building **get well food** such as homemade soup or fresh fruit salad. If you really want to speed their recovery, a **juicer** will provide them with instant, healthy, fresh-pressed fruit and vegetable juice, a cure in itself.

If your friend is shivery and cold, chatty phone calls and lengthy visits might not be appreciated. Instead a **hot water bottle** with a pretty cover might be just the thing to help speed them back to good health by warming away any feverish chills.
Conversely, a fever in the heat of summer is hard to bear. A **mineral water spray** (available from all good pharmacies) will help to cool them down.

When incapacitated with aches and pains, the last thing your chum wants to worry about is the dust piling up alongside the growing pile of used tissues and washing up. If a friend is in this predicament, **send round your cleaner** or go round yourself and **spring clean their home** from top to bottom.

Hospital is hell: it's boring, uncomfortable and the food is usually inedible. Satisfy the patient's craving for fresh food and the comforts of home with a **thermos of homemade soup** or a **bottle of mineral water** and an **attractive glass** and you will make their stay a little more bearable.

For girls, one of the most upsetting side effects of being in hospital is the lack of hair-washing facilities. After all, they want to look as good as they can for the stream of sympathetic visitors. If there's a hospital **hairdresser**, treat them to a wash and set or blow dry. With time on their hands, a visit from a **manicurist** would be a welcome surprise. (Hint: check the best time for this with the nursing staff.)

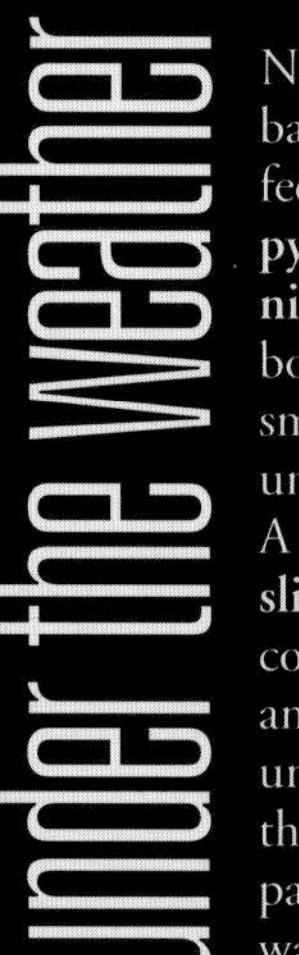

No matter how bad your chum feels, a pair of **silk pyjamas** or a **nightdress** is bound to bring a smile to their unhappy face. A new pair of **slippers** will complete the outfit and they will undoubtedly be the most attractive patient in the ward.

One sleepless night on foam-filled, polyester pillows is enough to drive any patient to distraction, so a get well gift which will really be appreciated is a **pair of sumptuous feather pillows**, complete with **linen cases.** (Hint: check that they're not allergic to feathers.)

If you are into alternative medicine but don't want to upset the hospital staff, no-one will object if you arrange for a **reflexologist** to come and give them a **healing foot massage.**

good scents

THE POWER *of* ***essential oils*** *to cure both emotional and physical ills is now widely recognised. A dab of oil on the pillow (see suggestions below), a burner with the appropriate oils or better still, for the recuperating patient,* ***an aromatherapy massage****, will do them the world of good. (Hint: care should be taken when using essential oils. Do not take them internally. If you are pregnant or have sensitive skin or any medical conditions, only use oils under supervision.)*

Basil - Relieves mental fatigue; aids memory and concentration (avoid during pregnancy). Clary sage - Anti-depressant and comforting. Jasmine - anti-depressant, and also an aphrodisiac. Lavender - Relaxing, relieves headaches, insomnia and burns. Neroli - For agitation and nervousness. Peppermint - Relieves nausea and sickness, digestive troubles, sunburn. Rose - Soothes emotional loss, counteracts negative feelings, relieves hangovers. Rosemary - Invigorating and stimulating; relieves aches and pains; increases potency; prevents baldness. Sandalwood - An aphrodisiac and sexual restorer; relieves sore throats; effective for skin problems. Tea tree - Antiseptic; relieves vaginal complaints, foot problems, insect bites and stings. Ylang Ylang - An aphrodisiac; relieves jet lag.

Feel good flowers: Cedar Tree - Strength. Camomile - Energy. Coreopsis - Always cheerful. Geranium, Scarlet - Comforting. Icelandic Moss -Health. Juniper - Protection. Shamrock - Light-heartedness

friends forever

MOST PEOPLE *at some time in their lives have a particularly close friend, the person who is best man or maid of honour at your wedding and is godparent to your first-born. This person, like a rare jewel, needs to be treasured. As a child, you might have suggested exchanging blood in order to become spiritual siblings; a more adult demonstration of the high regard in which you hold them could be one of the following gifts.*

FOR A dear friend who lives abroad, a representative idea of the close relationship you have could be the gift of a set of **your house keys** on a keyring engraved with the words "My home is your home". Whenever they come into the country they know they will have a place to lay their weary head. ❤ ♛

A TOUCHING token of your esteem, showing the confidence you have in the longevity of your friendship, would be to **bury a bottle** of champagne or good wine together, with the promise of sharing it a decade later. ❤

• AS A close friend of *Elton John* the highest accolade you can be given is a white orchid, symbolizing the purity of his unconditional friendship. ❤

A BRACELET is a traditional symbol of friendship. Make one that extra bit special by engraving a proverb or quotation on a disc to hang from it. For example "Love is blind; friendship closes its eyes", or "Fate chose your relations, you choose your friends". ❤

YOU SAY, hand on heart, that you will always be friends, so invest in a **pendant or bracelet** engraved with appropriate wording, then cut it in half so you can each wear your part. When the halves are put together, the promise will be complete. ❤

*Cut an engraved **bracelet** in half so you and your best friend can each wear a part.*

• **FOR HIS best friend's birthday, famed photographer *Herb Ritts* flew his friend's sister, whom he had not seen for many years, over from Australia. Upon her arrival, Herb wrapped her up and tied a huge ribbon around the precious parcel. The friend was delighted with the size of the mysterious gift but ecstatic when he discovered his sibling inside.❤**

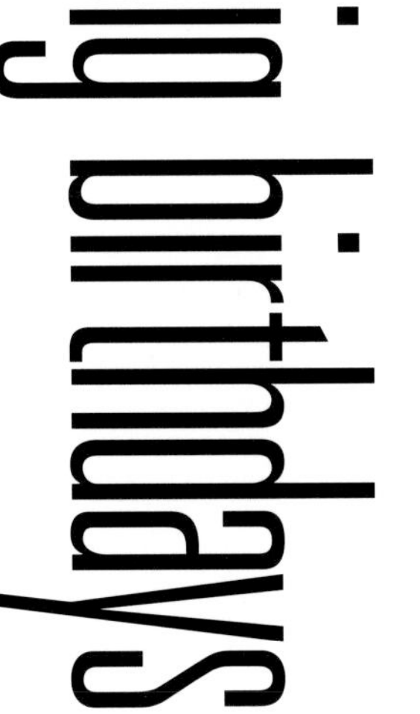

big birthdays

IT'S ALRIGHT *to let the odd birthday slip through the net, but there are those that should never be forgotten and, more importantly, celebrated to the full, marking the importance of the achieved milestone. For each triumphant arrival at the beginning of a new decade, as an alternative to the massively expensive present they would like but know they will probably not receive, what about the simple but sure-to-be appreciated gift of a number of items they'll regularly use, as lavish as you wish or can afford. For instance:*

For men:
20/30/40/50 golf/tennis balls, bottles of their favourite wine, socks, torches, keyrings

For women:
20/30/40/50 silk stockings, lipsticks, essential oils, cookbooks, flowers (roses or their favourite variety), scented candles

For anyone:
20/30/40/50 plant tags (for the keen gardener), truffles (for the chocoholic or, if you really want to lash out, for the gourmet, the real thing), CDs (for the music lover)

Coming of age:
18 or 21 classic books they should have read by now, a starter collection of 21 classic CDs, the appropriate number of driving lessons.

A VARIATION on the same theme would be to **throw a party** with 20/30/40/50 of everything: 30 friends, 30 bottles of wine or champagne, 30 bunches of flowers, 30 balloons etc.

When the halves are put together, the promise will be complete.❤

A selection of favourite games - like ***playing cards*** *- will contribute towards making their new house into a home.*❤

housewarming

In an ideal world most of us would love to have a garden, but a gardenless new home need not be flowerless as well because you, as a dear friend, could plant up **window boxes** with a seasonal array of blooms; it's a great idea even if there is a garden. (Hint: feeling flush? Get a florist or garden centre to plant them up for you.)

Alongside changing jobs and getting married, moving house is recognised as one of the three most traumatic events the average person experiences. Even for the most organised person, moving to a new home is a nightmare. The equilibrium of day-to-day life is upset; removal men and new neighbours have to be dealt with; decoration has to be decided upon. As a trusty friend, you can step in to help turn the nightmare into an exciting new beginning.

The decorators move out as they move in and everything smells of fresh paint and varnish. Help disguise the smell with some **scented candles** and **potpourri.**

OK, so your friend has the most fabulous pair of pewter candlesticks, the coolest CDs and a great line in ethnic crockery, but what about the home entertainment? Where is the **Monopoly**, the **chess set**, the **backgammon board**, **Trivial Pursuits**? Where are the **playing cards**? A selection of favourite games will contribute towards making their new house into a home.

No sooner have they settled down for their first quiet evening at home when there's a power cut. A **large box of candles** and **a rechargeable torch** are absolute essentials in any household.

Once your friends have spent their hard-earned cash on new household necessities, there is probably only a pittance left for the luxuries, so **personalised stationery** will be at the bottom of the list. However, you can answer their needs with a visit to the local printers to buy writing paper emblazoned with their new address.(Hint: postcards are less expensive.)

Most of their worldly possessions are still in packing cases, the place is upside-down but they are elated, because they have finally moved into their new home. Amid all this happy confusion, a clever moving-in present is simply to track down the local newsagent and arrange for a **daily newspaper delivery** for the first few weeks.

There's nothing more disorientating than moving to a completely different area. What your friends really need is a **Home Movers' Survival Kit** comprising a map of the area, a book on its history, a bus or train timetable, menus from local take-aways and important telephone numbers such as the doctor, the local hospital, police station and plumber. Make the gift even more special by inserting all the numbers in a new **address book.**

chaos

Living in the city is pretty dismal when it comes to seeing any form of vegetation. For friends who have moved to the concrete jungle, give them a taste of the country with an **indoor window box** planted up with herbs.

*As a parting gift, turn a photo of yourself and a friend into a **jigsaw**, take out the piece with her smiling face and add a note: "Missing you already".*

farewell

If you *have a friend who has decided to throw caution to the wind and pack their bags in search of excitement elsewhere, the chances are there will be a series of emotional goodbyes and declarations along the lines of "You are my best friend in the world", at the farewell parties given in their honour. Promises of daily correspondence and regular trips to visit them are extravagantly made as the euphoria of comradeship reaches its climax in the departure lounge.*

When a girl packs her suitcase, the one thing that out-weighs everything else is her cosmetic bag. She can cut down on shoes, clothing and jewellery, but to expect her to economize on face creams and make-up would be too much. It makes absolute practical sense, therefore, to fill **a vanity bag with travel-sized items.** (Hint: for a more practical finish, decant creams from glass pots and bottles to plastic ones.)

• When film director and writer *Bryan Forbes* arrived in Los Angeles on a business trip, he discovered to his surprise that his dear friend *Elton John* had organized an all-singing, all-dancing brass band to meet him off the airplane!

Turn a favourite photo of the two of you into **a jigsaw,** take out the piece with their smiling face and add a note: "Missing you already".

Spring a surprise at the airport and present your friend with **an upgraded ticket.** Band together with your gang of buddies to cover the cost and this will be a great way to say "Farewell". (Hint: you'll need to do a little sleuthing to organize this one, but once you know the flight and carrier your friend is booked with, deal direct with the airline to arrange the upgrading.)

come back soon

Whether a friend is off on a business trip or undertaking a total upheaval to another country, lighten up the tearful airport farewell scenes with the gift of **a boomerang**. The package will be comical enough to flip the mood from sobs to laughs and you'll be saying "Come back soon" in the sweetest possible way.

The hardest part of moving to a different part of the world, is leaving your friends behind. For a departing chum, compile **a photograph album** of all the good times you have spent together, so they may take you and the gang along for the ride. (Hint: a concertina fold-out album is the most mobile.)

Samuel Pepys kept one. Henry Kissinger kept one. Margaret Thatcher kept one. Give a parting friend the opportunity to keep one as well. Keep what? **A journal** in which to record their life whilst apart from things familiar. (Hint: for the lazy, substitute **a dictaphone** for the empty journal.)

missing you

When you arrive in a new country, it's not only disorientating on an emotional level but also dislocating as far as your whereabouts are concerned. Scanning the midnight skies to pinpoint the North Star is one option but a handy **map of the locality** might be more useful.

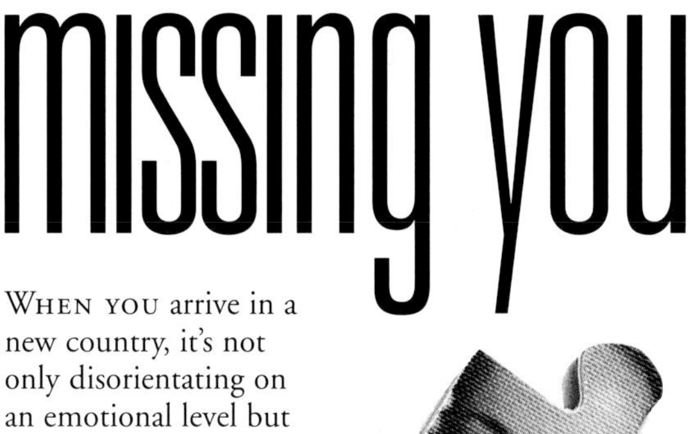

lucky numbers

So you know *their shoe size, all their nicknames and some of their most embarrassing moments. Even so, it can be very difficult to choose a sibling or a close friend the perfect present every time. If you're a bit stuck for inspiration, make use of your intimate knowledge of them by finding a present relevant to their astrological birth sign (see Start Chart page 89) or by calculating their lucky number. According to the laws of numerology, we all have these numbers, which can surmised from our date of birth and names. Either you can get their numerological chart worked out professionally, a fascinating present in itself, or you can work out the number yourself and choose a relevant present.*

Finding lucky numbers from dates
A lucky number must be between 1 and 9, so if they were born on any day from the 1st to the 9th of the month, that day is the lucky number. For higher dates, simply add the two digits together, for example, for someone born on the 22nd the number would be (2+2=4), the 13th would also be four (1+3=4). If a person is born on the 29th, add 2+9=11, then add 1+1=2 for their lucky number.

Finding lucky numbers from names
To find lucky numbers from someone's name use the following chart:

1	2	3	4	5	6	7	8	9
A	B	C	D	E	F	G	H	I
J	K	L	M	N	O	P	Q	R
S	T	U	V	W	X	Y	Z	

So the name John Brown is calculated as follows:

J O H N
1+ 6 + 8 + 5 = 20
2 + 0 = **2**

B R O W N
2 + 9 + 6 + 5 + 5 = 27

2 + 7 = **9**
9 + 2 = 11
1 + 1 = **2**

This formula opens up a whole new area of present-giving possibilities. For instance, if someone has the lucky number 2, a pair of anything, such as shoes, vases or tickets to the theatre, is a perfect gift.

seven

Number One:
One-armed bandit (slot machine)
Take them Formula One motor racing
Meet for lunch at 1 o'clock
Number 1 bestselling book/record
Something unique (antique, first edition, piece of china)
Unicycle
One-liner (a joke or joke book)

Number Two:
Tea for two somewhere really smart
Two English old pennies
Book a double room at a hotel
A pair of anything
Twice as many presents as usual

Number Three:
Three cheers
Three-dimensional object (sculpture)
Three-piece suit(e)
Grant them three wishes
A three-course meal

Number Four:
Four-leaf clover
Night in a four-poster bed
Four-pack of beer
Safari by four-wheeldrive
Something square
A plane ticket to the four corners of the world

Number Five:
Silver charm in the shape of a hand (five digits)
Book them into a five-star hotel
Take them shopping on Fifth Avenue, New York
Five-pointed star on chain

Number Six:
Six of the best - books, records, recipes
Half-a-dozen beautifully painted eggs
Set of six crystal glasses
Six months' subscription to the local health club
A set of hexagonal coloured pencils

Number Seven:
Charm bracelet symbolizing seven stages of life
Seven day holiday
Symbols of the seven virtues: faith, hope, charity, justice, fortitude, prudence and temperance
One week bus/rail pass

Number Eight:
Eight pieces of gold (after the Spanish coin)
Eight oysters
Dinner at 8 o'clock
Pair of skating boots (to make figure-of-eight)
Pool table

Number Nine:
Get them dressed up to the nines (a new dinner suit or evening dress)
A cat charm (nine lives)

Horses and Ponies - Sugar lumps, mints, apples, decorative brow band, set of grooming equipment, halter, leading rope, initialled rug, saddle bags.

Fish - Gourmet fish food, treasure trove, boyfriend or girlfriend, sparkling pebbles, fish tank, pond, underwater camera.

Rabbits, hamsters, and other furry beasts - Lettuce leaves, sunflower seeds, exercise wheel, straw or sawdust, hutch with style.

pets

When we *think of friends, the image that springs to mind is of the two-legged variety, but we should never forget our winged, four-legged, furry or finned companions, who don't answer back, who listen to hours of repetitive chatter without getting a glazed, bored look in their eyes and who love us unconditionally, warts and all.* If a friend of yours is the besotted owner of such a creature, the way to impress them is to **suck up to their pet**. The following gift list is dedicated to scaled, feathered or furry friends: **Dogs** - Bone, dog chocs, studded collar, mackintosh, duvet, course at dog-training school, basket, day in the pet parlour. **Cats** - Mouse (toy), carton of thick cream, fresh fish, catmint, identity tag, day in the pet parlour, scratching post, diamanté collar

Birds - Nuts and raisins, swing, bell, perch, bath, tree branch or twig, feathered friend, gilded cage.

There are people, such as our families, long-time partners and close friends, with whom we have exchanged gifts from the year dot. Although you can get away with binoculars of used lavatory rolls and telephones of yoghurt cartons and string for so long, there comes a time when this type of handicraft simply will not do. Once we start earning a living - whether it's washing the family car or running a multi-national corporation - it is appropriate to begin spending some of that hard-won cash on others as well as ourselves. A thoughtful present bought with our own savings will surely meet with a round of applause.

Unfortunately, the people to whom we give year after year are probably the most difficult for whom to find presents. They test our imagination to the limit. How often have you thought "Oh no. What shall I give Mum this time? I have done the books, the gardening tools, the head scarves, the furry slippers etc... What now?" It's a tough one. However, help is at hand, so read on.

people you give to
year after year...
after...
year

brothers & sisters

As children *you fought like cats and dogs but, at the end of the day, blood is thicker than water and the rivalry between siblings usually evolves into a unique bond that is cherished throughout their lives.*

Your brothers and sisters are grown up and married with kids. Parents can easily take their children for granted, forgetting to record their early years except with the usual out-of-focus, badly composed holiday snapshots, thereby missing each delightful stage as they change with the years. As a favourite aunt or uncle, you could take it upon yourself to commission an annual or five-yearly **portrait or photograph of your nephews and nieces** to remind their proud parents how angelic they really were.❤

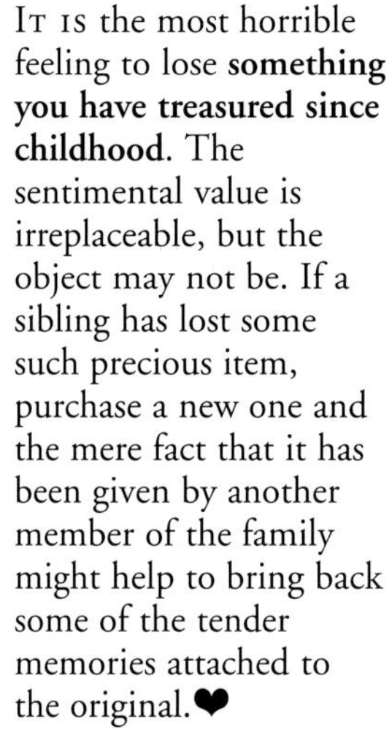

It is the most horrible feeling to lose **something you have treasured since childhood**. The sentimental value is irreplaceable, but the object may not be. If a sibling has lost some such precious item, purchase a new one and the mere fact that it has been given by another member of the family might help to bring back some of the tender memories attached to the original.❤

You might now live in another area, or even country, to your sibling. As you know their taste so well, why not start a collection for them through **mail order**. It could be anything from old 45 rpm records, sheet music, model cars, specialist books, classical CDs or coins.❤

If you were smart enough to have kept any **letters** written to you by your brother or sister, an amusing idea is to **send them back** sporadically. The appalling spelling and non-existent grammar will provide them with hours of amusement as would a bound folder containing their **old school reports.**❤

You shared a bedroom, a gene pool and the raucous pleasure of dancing around the sitting room, singing into a hairbrush and pretending to be the Rolling Stones, Blondie or Nirvana. Relive your rock 'n' roll memories by giving your sibling **a compilation of those vintage pop songs.**❤

If you feel that you have drifted apart from your sibling and want to shore up the relationship, think of a present that will rekindle the family ties. What do you have in common? Your parents of course! Find **something that symbolizes both your parents** and set it in a beautiful frame. It could be photographs taken in the early days of their romance or of them as children. Or it could be a memento from their respective childhoods - a letter, a prize rosette or a photograph of the house they grew up in. Surely you must have some **old photographs of you all as children**. Dig them out, make a selection of the funniest and have them framed as a photographic montage, which in turn can be colour photocopied and sent to each of your brothers and sisters.❤

treasures

A recent visit to your married sibling reveals a half-crazed parent, exhausted from lack of sleep, maddened by hyperactive kids and desperate for some time alone with spouse. Do them a favour and take the children away for a day or two, thereby granting them a welcome **weekend of peace and tranquillity.**

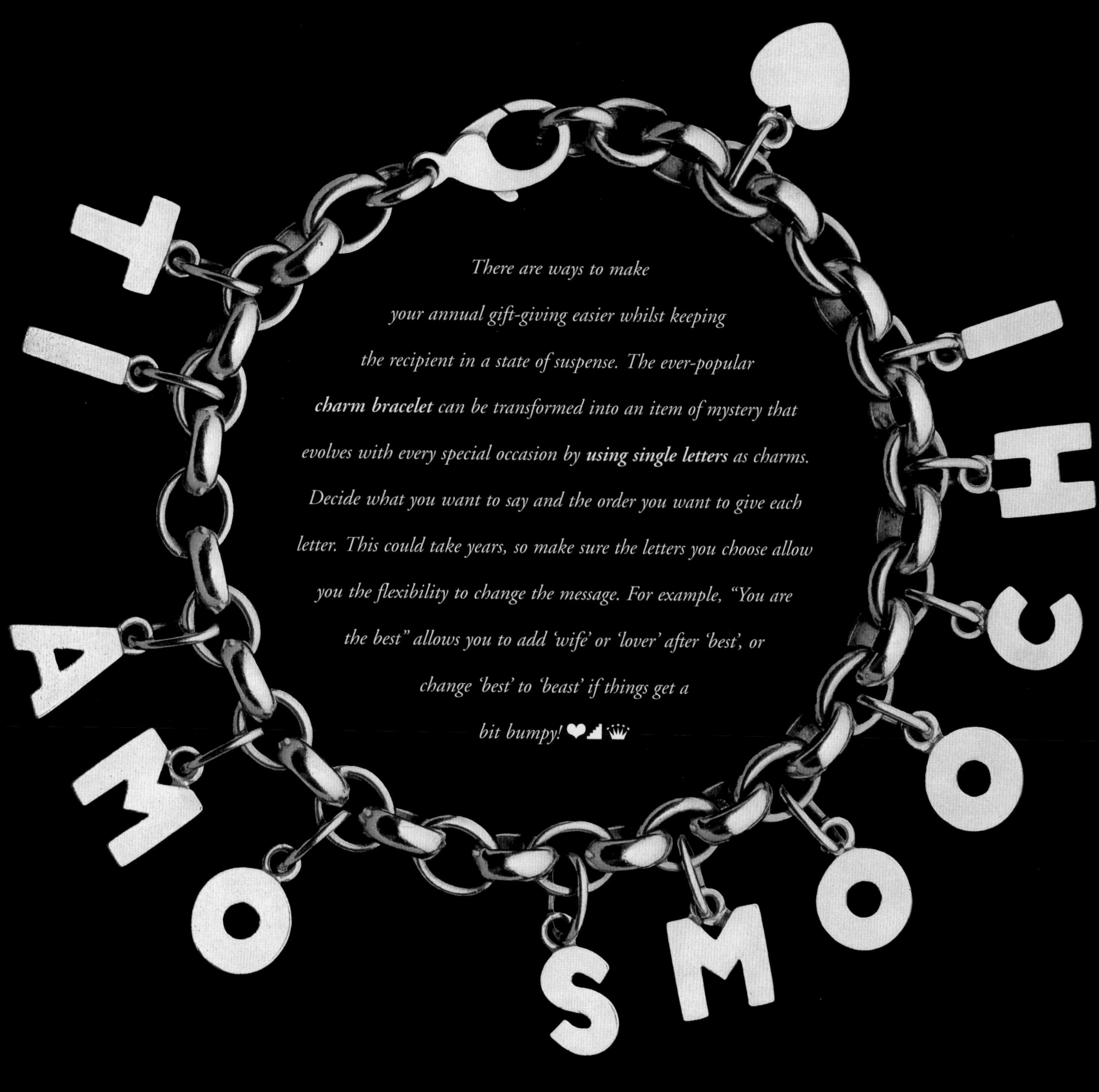

There are ways to make your annual gift-giving easier whilst keeping the recipient in a state of suspense. The ever-popular ***charm bracelet*** *can be transformed into an item of mystery that evolves with every special occasion by* ***using single letters*** *as charms. Decide what you want to say and the order you want to give each letter. This could take years, so make sure the letters you choose allow you the flexibility to change the message. For example, "You are the best" allows you to add 'wife' or 'lover' after 'best', or change 'best' to 'beast' if things get a bit bumpy!*

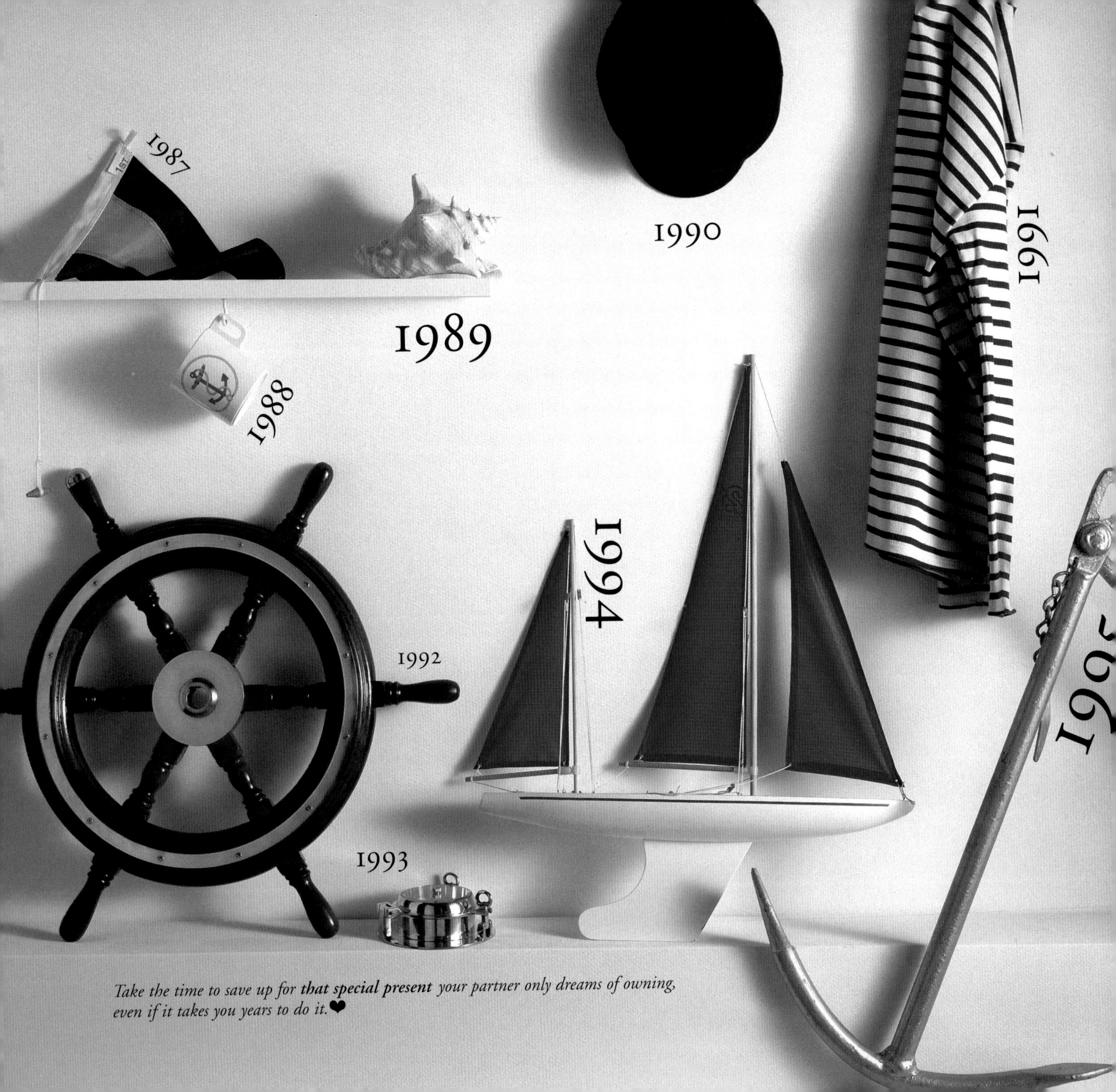

*Take the time to save up for **that special present** your partner only dreams of owning, even if it takes you years to do it.*❤

partners

Valentine's *presents, birthday presents, anniversary presents, Christmas presents, spur-of-the-moment presents... In a relationship, just keeping track of all the occasions is taxing enough, let alone thinking of something original to give them.*

Your lover knows that his or her desire for a gold watch is way outside your budget, but you know how important that item is to them. Under these circumstances, take the time to save up for **that special present** your partner only dreams of owning, even if it takes you years to do it. For the interim celebrations make sure they know you are up to something by giving cryptic clues as gifts. For example, if you are saving for a boat, you can give anything from a captain's hat, or a rubber ring to a T-shirt with the name of the boat on it. If it's a trip to India they have set their heart on, provide them with a sari, a book on Indian cookery, a guide book, to be followed ultimately by the wallet containing air ticket and hotel bookings.❤

Have a **favourite board game** made up in special materials. One way of doing this would be to go to the end-of-year show at the local art college and commission a talented young artist to make up an unusual chess set or Scrabble board or get a woodwork student to design a wonderful inlaid backgammon board.❤

They may drive you to distraction sometimes, but you love them. You love them because they make you laugh. You love them because they sing off-key in the shower. You love them for their enthusiasm for life. There are so many reasons why we adore our partners, in fact, that it is a delightful idea to **record a reason why** for each year you have been together, adding a new one annually in subsequent years. These can be **engraved in a precious metal, studded in gems, carved in wood or hand-written on a piece of notepaper**. The choice is yours.❤

The gift of a **cushion** is a classic present that your loved one will see and cherish every day. Depending on your abilities, you could make the **cushion cover** yourself or commission it. Choose your own design and ask for initials or a message to be embroidered on it.❤

parents

Parents are *impossible present beneficiaries. The older you get, the harder they become to please and surprise. However, just remember that you know them better than anyone else, you understand their little quirks and eccentricities and have inside information on their interests and hobbies. So, even if they have received every piece of literature on their special interest, you can always encourage a new hobby or give something entirely different that they would never have expected in their wildest dreams.*

If your parents have a garden, you can't go wrong by giving them **a tree** or a **rose bush** to love and nurture. It will always be precious to them and they will think of you with every twig it grows and every flower that blooms.❤

It is amazing how much clutter our parents seem to accumulate over the years. Their cupboards bulge with piles of memorabilia precious only to them, such as old love letters, our baby clothes, grandma's costume jewellery and grandpa's pipe collection. However, if you asked them to dig out that photograph of you and your sister cooking mud pies, the chances are that the next Ice Age will have come and gone by the time they manage to unearth it. With this in mind, a perfect gift for them would be **a trunk** filled with empty boxes labelled with tags saying: **Box of Secrets, Box of Memories, Box of Love, Treasure Trove, Baby Box** etc. Alternatively, a more practical path could be pursued with the same trunk packed with **a sewing box, tool box, cigar box, fishing tackle box, jewellery box** etc.

Organize ***a trip down memory lane*** *for your parents. Discreetly find out where they stayed on their honeymoon and pre-book the same room.*❤

mother &

As you know your parents inside out, you are in a unique position to enhance their enjoyment of life by giving them a gift that is tailored to their own favourite pastime. This might be making jams and relishes, pickling onions or bottling wine, each finished item requiring **a specific label**. These labels for their home-made delicacies make a simple but smart and practical gift if professionally printed. You are the best judge as to whether **a drawing of their house** or **a caricature of the family** is the best choice to illustrate the label, then add the appropriate words.

You've probably kept your parents awake for a large chunk of their lives. As a newborn, you will have wailed the nights away and as a wayward teenager they will have worried themselves into insomnia as you failed to return from the youth club disco on time. It's time now to ensure their uninterrupted nights of sleep with a **herb pillow** or **an essential oil burner** and a specially concocted **sleep oil** made up from a mixture of rosemary and lavender oils.

There comes a point when all children have to leave the nest and, for parents, this can be a distressing and worrying time. To compensate for their loss and to keep your parents in touch with your life, **chronicle your year** by making an album that not only holds photos, but also features mementos of your adventures. By labelling each album with the year, this annual present will become a visual record of your life.

How often do you thank your lucky stars that God gave you the parents you have, for their constant support through the ups and downs of your life? But have you ever really tried to show them how much you appreciate them? One way of giving them a token of your love and gratitude would be to give them a **garden bench dedicated to them from you** - a wonderful gesture which will last a lifetime. Either you could contact the park authority who will tell you how this can be done in your local park or, if this proves too expensive, you can buy a bench, get a brass plaque made and attached, then secretly place it in your parents' own garden. Cover the gift, then lead them out for the grand unveiling ceremony.

father

How many times have we been subjected to stories of our birth in graphic detail? It is astonishing, too, how parents can remember and like to remind us of the gruesome details of our early physical appearance. Ah... but do they recall what was happening in the rest of the world on our (or their) birth date? Doubtful. Well, here is an opportunity to **source a newspaper** from that momentous day (and those of our siblings) and have the front pages made up into **a set of table mats.** (Hint: ring a company that specializes in old newspapers or call the newspaper in question who will send you a copy.)

trip down memory lane

Transform your parents into a courting couple again by organizing **a trip down memory lane** to the place they went for their honeymoon. This can be made really special if you can discreetly find out where they stayed and pre-book the same room.

Queue up for **tickets to the hot new show** in town so you can give your parents the best seats in the house on the opening night. Oh, and if you have a natural aversion to queues or simply loathe hanging around waiting, just remember how many hours they've devoted to you in the past. So get on and hit that queue!

godchild

IF YOU are lucky enough to be a godparent, you'll also be aware that you may end up being the impressionable child's role model. So why not encourage them now in an interest you can share during those teenage crisis years? The gift of a **year's lessons in their favourite sport** would enable you to spend time together outdoors, either playing it with them or watching them compete as a result of the prowess they have achieved.

AS WELL as being a worthy role model, part of the reason you were no doubt chosen as godparent was for your desire to invest in the future of your godchild. You can do this financially by opening a **savings account or insurance policy** on their behalf. Alternatively, the gift of knowledge is priceless, so **a set of encyclopedias or a CD-Rom encyclopedia** could prove a fabulous encouragement to their education.

BY INITIATING a collection for your godchild, you will never have to worry about what to give for subsequent birthdays and special occasions. A **beautifully bound book** with a personalized Ex Libris label could be the start of a priceless library. A fine **bottle of wine** with ageing qualities can be joined in subsequent years by others to create a wine cellar. A **porcelain cup and saucer** will grow into a tea or coffee set. Even toys, such as **teddy bears or dolls,** if not played with too much whilst they are children, will become collectors' items in future years. **Coins or stamps** are both fun to collect and educational. If the child develops an interest, he or she can add to the collection as they grow older, but failing that they will have a ready-made investment which they can sell.

*For your godchild, start a **collection** at birth which you add to year after year, occasionally giving a token present as well.*

Celebrities pave the way for us ordinary folk to be more aware of our charitable obligations. Many of us only remember the needy at Christmas. What about the rest of the year? A present with a bit more meaning than most would be to **sponsor a child's education or welfare** in a troubled part of the world, or **adopt an animal**, either an orphan baby or one of an endangered species, for example. Alternatively, make your godchild a **member of an environmental charity** which will broaden their knowledge of this worthwhile area.

It doesn't have to be diamonds, pearls can also be a girl's very good friend. Give your goddaughter one for every birthday so she can string together a **pearl necklace or bracelet** in the course of time.

Instead of giving a series of gifts over the years, why not buy **one big present** that your godchild can appreciate when he or she is older. This might be an antique that you yourself have inherited, or the work of an artist who is just making his/her name.

You will need the help of the child's parents for this one; ask them to keep his or her **first shoes**, then get them **cast in bronze**. This will make a unique ornament to be given to them when they are fully grown, symbolizing their first steps towards adulthood.

collectors' item

Encourage your godchild to develop a wanderlust by decorating their room with **maps of the world**. It's cheaper than most wallpaper and more interesting than paint.

25

family christmas

CHRISTMAS *is a time of festivity, giving, family reunions and over-indulgence. It is a time to implement time-honoured family traditions, but it is also a time of exhausting preparation and of racking one's brains for gift ideas that will be appreciated by everyone from your great aunt to your newborn nephew.*

To reduce the stress levels inevitably heightened by this taxing time of year, here are a few suggestions to make your next Christmas the best you have ever had. Do you remember the excitement of opening the windows of your Advent Calendar? In Scandinavia it is traditional to receive a small Advent gift on each day leading up to Christmas, with the biggest and the best saved for the big day. For the Ultimate Family Christmas, we have expanded on this theme and compiled a list of Advent presents which incorporates all the necessities for the festive celebrations ahead.

1st - **Christmas Cards**
2nd - **Sellotape**
3rd - **A ball of string**
4th - **Ribbon**
5th - **Name tags**
6th - **Scissors**
7th - **Gift wrap**

8th - **Xmas Tree**
9th - **Decorations**
10th - **A bag of nuts**
11th - **Xmas Pudding**
12th - **Crackers**
13th - **A lucky charm**
14th - **Candles**

15th - **A family game**
16th - **Champagne**
17th - **Soft drinks**
18th - **A wreath**
19th - **A selection of hangover cures**
20th - **Chocolates**

9

21st - **Camera film**
22nd - **Edible delicacies**
23rd - **Ingredients for Christmas meal**
24th - **An empty stocking**
25th - **Big surprise**

12

The Ultimate Affiliation Stocking

Board game
Book of romantic poetry or special thoughts
Empty book with beautiful paper
Chocolate truffles to share
Cook books
Cuddly toy
Family photograph or frame
Homemade cookies
Pot-pourri
Genuine beeswax candles
Fruit and nuts
Scented oil or soap
(Everything beautifully wrapped)

The Ultimate Achievement Stocking

Any new fad
Anything designer-labelled
Beautiful bronze front door knocker
Calling cards
Car mascot
Cashmere socks
Desk toys
Good photo of themselves
Magic tricks
Monogrammed pen or pencil
Personalised stationery
Tickets to the hottest show in town
The latest and most talked-about book
Top-of-the-range fountain pen

The Ultimate Power Stocking

Any electrical appliance
Army knife
Bag of gold chocolate money
Pocket calculator
Credit-card holder
Exotic fruit
Intellectually challenging book
New diary
Overnight bag
Pocket-sized sewing kit or manicure set
Silk socks or stockings
Small pocket torch
Solitaire
State-of-the-art desk lamp
Travel alarm clock
Wallet

Surprise a fishing fanatic - instead of putting a new rod and flies under the tree, why not hang them on it.

THE DAYS *of manic preparation have now come to a head, it's Christmas Day and time to eat, drink and be merry. Look forward to flying wrapping paper and delighted exclamations when your friends and family open the ideal gifts you have chosen for them. Here are a few suggestions for the sports supporter and gifts that are suitable for the entire family.*

sports maniacs

Football Fan: Rattle or horn, football, supporter's hat and scarf, banner inscribed with the home team's name, signed photograph of their football hero (available from fan club), strips of the team they support, compilation video of great football highlights, tickets to the next important match.

Golfing Groupie: Tees, golfing shoes, baseball cap or bobble golfing hat, golfing gloves, belt for purse and tees, a dozen balls, subscription to a golfing magazine, umbrella, diamond design sweater with matching socks.

Fishing Fanatic: Subscription to an angling magazine, outsize umbrella, flies or spinners suitable for their favourite area, waterproofs and waders, fishing permit for the local river, new state-of-the-art fishing rod, landing net, hip flask.

Head over Heels about Horses: Whip, riding gloves, books on horses, tickets to an equestrian event, riding hat or stetson, riding or cowboy boots, hacking jacket, course of riding lessons, drawing or china statuette of a horse.

The Ultimate Family Christmas Presents: The family's names or photographs printed on personalised place mats, a video camera to record The Ultimate Family Christmas, a set of blank videos to avoid squabbles over television programmes, a board game, disposable cameras, a vast tin of biscuits, someone to do the washing up, a book of carols, a set of classic Christmas films, a hamper, a box of pencils engraved with all the family's names, a 2000-piece jigsaw puzzle.

xmas tree

Tree Presents: These are little token gifts that can be hung on the tree and opened before retiring to bed. For the sake of the tree, the less they weigh the better, for example: **pencils**, **handkerchiefs**, **chocolate money or liqueur chocolates**, **hair ornaments**, **bubble bath or shampoo sachets**. Although they are just a gesture, they work wonders in bribing children to go to bed on time!

The Christmas Secret: Would you consider freshly picked roses from the garden on Christmas Day an impossible wish to be granted? Well, we know something you may not. Follow these instructions carefully... In the latter part of September, pick twelve tightly shut rosebuds with long stalks. Place them in hot water for one hour, then wrap them in cotton wool before putting them in a long tin box. Seal the box with strong adhesive tape and bury it in a flower bed, 18 ins/45 cm below ground. On Christmas morning, unearth them and plunge them into water. They will open swiftly, but be warned, after six hours their fresh beauty will wither and die. Still, at least you can truthfully say, "I got these out of the garden, just this morning!"

As a rule we spend more time with the people with whom we work than with our family and friends. However, unless you are the boss, you have no input in choosing your colleagues and have to live with them irrespective of whether you like them or not.

During the course of time, they become akin to an extended family, with the same requirement to recognise their birthdays, engagements etc.

On top of these anniversaries, there is the continual struggle to gain allies in the workplace, get a promotion or prevent being sacked.

Gifts work wonders for all the above scenarios. Remembering a birthday or bringing back a holiday souvenir will forge friendships, a carefully chosen present for an important client could win you the contract and a promotion. But be warned, all eyes in the office will be focusing on your offering. The line between blatant bribery and getting it right is very fine. You must never underestimate competitiveness in the working environment, so if you want to leap up the corporate ladder, study this chapter with care.

someone you
work with

Make an office birthday extra special by ordering a novelty cake that represents an interest of the birthday boy or girl - even if it is dieting!

birthday

A colleague, *employee or boss's birthday is a vital occasion to put in the office diary. Remembering and celebrating your colleagues' birthdays preserves a harmonious mood as well as creating a welcome moment of diversion in the daily routine. We all benefit from a bout of frivolity and appreciate an excuse to get away from the stresses and strains of work. The first task is to establish the actual day of birth: pour over the horoscope column in the newspaper with your work mate during a coffee break. Once you know the month, you can be on the alert for further clues as to the exact date.*

the boss

Surprising as it may seem, your immediate superior also needs reassurance and may crave the affection and approval of his or her staff. If you and your colleagues feel you've got a great boss, then show him or her by having a **photograph** taken of all of you raising a cheer and have it **framed to sit on their desk** alongside the family photos.❤

Most of us have a tendency to **doodle** on the nearest piece of blank paper, in a meeting or whilst on the phone. Pinch these 'works of art' from the birthday boy or girl's desk and **frame them**, or make them into a **paper-weight** by setting them in Perspex.❤ ♛

Another essential for the inveterate note sender or doodler is plenty of paper to indulge their habit. Have some **personalised stationery** made up for them, perhaps 'From the desk of (name)' for the would-be high flyer, or featuring an appropriately pompous photograph. (Hint: catch them by surprise with the Polaroid and make use of the office photocopier.) ♛

colleagues

One advantage of organizing a birthday present for a colleague is that all the potential givers are in the same place. For a special birthday, club together to **give them an evening out,** or nip off and buy that **article of clothing** they were drooling over in their favourite designer shop.❤

On the first day of Christmas my secretary gave to me: **an initialled top-of-the-range diary.** (And it wasn't just because knowing that I would enjoy filling the dates in would make her life easier!) ♛

If you listen to music from the **local radio station** in your work place, why not have a **dedication** made to the birthday boy or girl in your office. Listen to the team squeal (with delight or embarrass-ment) as your favourite DJ mentions your company and colleague live on-air!❤

A must for every birthday celebration is the cake. Make it extra special by ordering a **novelty cake** that represents an interest or a dream of the birthday boy or girl. If he is fanatic about Italian sports cars, an edible Ferrari can be speedily arranged; if she is always talking about retiring to a country cottage, this is easier baked than done, complete with grazing horse and barking hound. (Hint: remember to take a photograph before cutting into it, so that they have more than crumbs left the next day.)❤ ♛

with many thanks

KNOWING *when to reward people you work with is a crucial element in maintaining a productive and successful business. A job well done should receive recognition. Look after your staff and you will reap the rewards of loyalty and higher productivity.*

BURNING the midnight oil in hours of overtime has obviously taken its toll and they are looking distinctly pale and wan. It's definitely time to relax the pressure and give them a break. A large gift-wrapped box containing this rather odd combination of items could do the trick and put the smile back on their face: **a pair of cashmere socks, a bottle of vintage claret and the latest bestselling novel.** Present it to them, along with a card saying: "We really appreciate your hard work. You deserve to go home, put your feet up, have a drink and get into a good book."

YOU MAY *feel one of two reactions when a colleague is promoted. One: genuine happiness for them and their achievement; two: it should have been me! Let us focus here on the response to an associate's meteoric rise to corporate fame. If you work for them, you will want to ensure that they have your interests at heart and if you now work alongside them, it is best to be friends. Start off on the right footing by giving a congratulatory gift.*

THE BETTER the promotion, the larger his or her new office is likely to be. That well-thumbed calendar, the wish-you-were-here travel poster or the silly office snapshots will no longer be suitable in this august new setting. Club together with your colleagues and buy the newly promoted one a **beautifully framed print or painting** to hang on their wall.

££ bonus

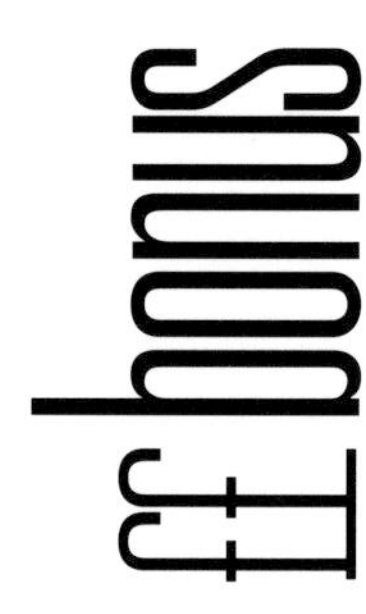

"WHAT GOOD boys and girls you have been". Remember how those words would thrill you as an innocent young school child? Well, rustle up that nostalgic, award-winning symbol, the **gold star**, but take it a step on from the school's paper variety. **Star-shaped gifts** come in all shapes and sizes, from earrings and pendants to candlesticks or mirrors.

• SUPER STAR tennis ace *Martina Navratilova* was rewarded with a bit more than a pat on the back for her amazing achievements, when she retired from the professional tennis circuit. Much to her surprise and delight, the organizers of the final tournament and her tennis friends presented her with the ultimate golden handshake, in the form of a glittering Harley Davidson bike.

IF YOUR crew have performed brilliantly as a team, have a batch of **team T-shirts** made up for them. They will be worn with pride!

IT WAS a close run thing. The business was up against its most professional competitors. You knew that your work force had to pull off something pretty incredible to win this contract, and today you have just heard that all that hard work has paid off. The company is back at the head of its field and there's no stopping you now. Those that executed this fantastic achievement deserve a reward proportionate to their success. Contact a local jeweller and commission **customised cuff-links** that symbolize the accomplishment.

congratulations

BEING promoted generally makes people happier and prouder than getting a pay rise. Show your enthusiasm for their achievement by giving a present worthy of the occasion (it might be your turn next time around). **A director's chair** with the lucky person's name on it is slightly tongue-in-cheek, but will nevertheless probably be secretly admired and take pride of place in their new office.

THE RED plastic **desk accessories** were all very well when they were a minute minion, but now that they have been elevated to a position of power, it's time to exchange the shoddy pen holder, letter rack and blotter for a smart new leather model which will reflect their new status in the heirarchy.

A job well done should receive recognition; reward your hard-working staff with ***customised cuff-links*** *that symbolize their accomplishment.*

keep them happy

It may not *be home or sweet, but the fact is you spend at least eight hours a day there, so your office environment has to be almost as important as your home surroundings. Keep your colleagues, staff or boss sweet by making the office a place which is conducive to fulfilling work and concentration.*

In order to keep up the high rate of production, you've got to allow the workers some moments of frivolous amusement. What better than going out on their behalf to place a series of **bets on the big sporting event** that's coming up? Hide the betting slips in attractive cards and neatly write the names of your colleagues on the envelopes. On the big day the office TV will be on and all work stations abandoned as the race/match takes place, everyone holding their breath with excited anticipation, safe in the knowledge that even if they lose it hasn't cost them a cent for their few minutes' worth of fun.❤

Ahhhhh… the smell of freshly ground coffee. You can't beat it. Unfortunately, most of us have to make do with a cup of the insipid instant variety on a workaday basis. If you want higher, caffeine-induced productivity, look sharp and invest in **a state-of-the-art real coffee-making machine.**❤

Once the management has provided the wherewithal to make it, you can provide the crocks from which to drink it. Many of your colleagues will have acquired nicknames (though they may not be aware of it), so liven up that Monday morning shot of caffeine by having a set of **personalised mugs** appear in the office kitchen. Leave them guessing as to which is meant for whom.❤

• WHEN THE 'Big Seven' met in Naples for the 1994 summit, present-fever erupted with everyone trying to outdo everyone else in their impressive choice. One of the most original gifts was presented by ***Silvio Berlusconi,*** then Prime Minister of Italy, who bought a personally selected **tie** for everyone attending, with a handwritten note stressing the special 'ties' between his country and that of the recipient.❤

THE STERILE, functional atmosphere of the office can be immensely improved by the scent and sight of fresh flowers or a well-nurtured plant on every desk and in all the meeting rooms. Rather than relying on the staff to undertake the chore of buying and watering and risk the unhappy sight of drooping, dying blooms, have your local florist provide **fresh flowers each week.** ❤

ANOTHER way to help them through those longer days than usual whilst a crisis deadline is looming over them, when they have to leave home at dawn and return in the late hours, is to take away the strain of travel. Paying for a **taxi, chauffeur-driven car or first-class travelcard to and from work** for an allotted time would be a real luxury present that would certainly be appreciated and could well pay dividends.

GIVE THEM a day off with a pre-paid session at the **hair-dresser** or **gym**, a calming facial at the **beauty salon**, tickets to a **sporting event** or the latest **movie, concert or show.**❤

MAY
JUNE
Keep your workforce in the peak of health by providing them with a ***Stressbuster Pack*** *containing a year's supply of vitamin pills.*
AUG

crisis management

THERE COMES *a time in every office's life when the atmosphere is one of desperation and morale is at an all-time low. At this point something must be done immediately to ward off the impending nervous breakdowns and get everyone back on an even keel.*

IN TIMES of trauma there is nothing like a cup of hot sweet tea. However, overdosing on caffeine stimulates the nervous system and, in this case, will only help activate the sweeping hysteria. Rush round to the nearest health store and replace the tension-boosting beverage with a selection of soothing **herbal infusions.**

pressure

ALL BUSINESSES are subject to tight deadlines that necessitate intense, mind-bending bouts of ridiculously hard work. One way to wind everyone down would be to arrange a **group membership to the nearest gym** where they can go to work off all the tension. Alternatively, **call in a masseur** to lay a pair of healing hands on the knotted shoulders of your workforce.

IN A WORK crisis, the best thing to do is to bond; try to remember that you're all in the same boat. Encourage the team spirit by buying **lottery tickets** for the whole office. You can stave off a crisis, at least momentarily, by fantasizing on how you'll all spend your winnings.

YOU'RE stressed out, you just can't cope, if one more person asks 'just a really small favour', you're going to explode. Stress and exhaustion reduce the immune system and lead inevitably to illness, so if you want to maintain your team at the peak of bouncing health, provide them with a **Stressbuster Pack** containing an appropriate variety of vitamin pills and herbal tonics. No work place should be without one.

AN OFFICE is a bit like a marriage, there are good times and bad, riches and poverty and, like a marriage, you need to work at it to keep it on the right track. If you are going through a bad patch, it is time to think of some little gesture to cheer everyone up. Comfort food is what they need, so play mother and have **cakes delivered on a Friday**. Could be just what the doctor ordered.

RESEARCH has shown that certain aromas can alleviate stress and so increase productivity in the work place. What better gift to your stressed-out colleagues than an **aromatherapy oil burner or fan** to keep the atmosphere sweet?

Key essential oils for the work place are:

Monday morning blues
Cajaput - Focusing in the present
Jasmine - Uplifting

Any Morning
Lemon - Refreshing/wake-up
Bergamot - Good mood

After that working lunch
Rosemary - Stimulant
Peppermint - Concentration

All stressed out
Bensoin - Soothing the nerves
Neroli - Stress reliever
Ylang Ylang - Confidence giver

Winding down at the end of the day
Lavender - Relaxing

culture shock

With all the good intentions in the world, you can still make a crashing corporate faux pas. Sending an inappropriate gift to an important foreign client could prove fatal to your relationship. Always check the company's corporate protocol before sending any gift at all; some large companies have strict policies on accepting gifts; and don't forget the import duties when giving items to people abroad. If in doubt, check with the embassy of the country concerned, they should be able to help. Finally, when dealing with foreign business associates, you must consider the cultural taboos. There are books on the subject and once again the embassy will be able to help out if in doubt, but here are some key areas to be aware of:

Middle East: In the Middle East alcohol is out. Similarly, anything resembling the female form. An initialled linen handkerchief is, usually, a well-received token, but unfortunately not in this case. To someone from the Middle East a handkerchief denotes tears and sadness, so they will think you are the bearer of bad news - not exactly the right mood to create for that all-important business meeting.

Japan: In Japan, white is the colour of death, so think twice before presenting your important Japanese client with a gift delicately wrapped in white tissue paper. A set of four crystal whisky glasses might seem like the perfect token to a nation who adore this Scottish spirit. Wrong again: the number 4, to a Japanese or Korean, ranks with 13 as a 'bad luck' number. Beware, too, of those innocent-looking hunting prints or watercolours of the pastoral English countryside. Any sign of a fox signifies 'fertility', while a badger signifies 'cunning' - both of which would be giving your guest quite the wrong message.

China: Tick-tock, tick-tock, what about a travel clock? No. Unfortunately the word 'clock' in Chinese has morbid, funereal connotations and would be all wrong.

India: White, as in Japan, is the colour of death, so steer clear. Be careful, too, of presenting your Indian client with a leather-bound desk set or initialled briefcase: for Hindus the cow is a sacred animal; pig-, sheep- and goat-skin are perfectly acceptable.

Europe: Not understanding the subtle meaning behind your floral tribute can lead you into trouble: never take red and white flowers to an unfortunate colleague in hospital as they are considered unlucky; red roses are a universal sign of passion and love (not quite the done thing in the work situation); chrysanthemums and white lilies are both symbols of death. Never give Irish whisky to a Scot, nor Scotch whisky to an Irishman. Never give food or perfume to the French - they are connoisseurs of food and cuisine, after all.

people you don't know

If you *have important customers coming into town, you'll want to impress them, but not knowing them personally makes choosing the right gift difficult. Using the psychological formula, here are some suggestions for each group:*

POWER GIFTS: (for those Special Star Clients) A **car with driver** or **access to your cab account** for the duration of their stay in your city/country. **Lend them your secretary** (a great sacrifice that can't fail to impress). Call up their office and brush up on your knowledge of their taste buds. Arrange for **a hamper** of their personal penchants to be waiting for them upon arrival. The use of **a laptop computer** throughout their stay. If they have a favourite sport, like golf or tennis, present them with a **championship racket** or a top quality **set of clubs.**

ACHIEVEMENT GIFTS: (for the Go-getting Executive) A **map of the city** with lists of the best restaurants, bars and nightclubs. An **initialled bath robe**, waiting for them in their hotel room. A battery-powered **travel reading light** for those long-haul work sessions. A top-of-the-range **briefcase**, with a combination lock to indicate the importance of their load. Tickets to an **exclusive show**, or better still a charity gala premiere. **Temporary membership** of the most exclusive golf/tennis club or gym. On their flight home, **arrange for champagne to be served** as a sign to their fellow passengers of their great importance. Anything **leather** and **initialled**. A **pen or watch** (as top-of-the-range as you can afford), engraved with the date and a personal message.

AFFILIATION GIFTS: (for Long-standing Business Connections) Invite your client to bring his family and, while you're discussing business, **arrange for the family to be taken shopping/sightseeing**. Get a **photograph** taken of yourself and the person in question. Have it framed and send it to him at the conclusion of your successful negotiations. A set of crystal **glasses and a decanter**, engraved with two hands clasped together, will symbolize your friendship and business bond. Last, but by no means least, remember that this group needs to belong; the ultimate gift for this person would be an invitation to join you and yours for **an informal family dinner**.

chinese horoscopes

FOR COLLEAGUES *as well as personal friends, gifts relating to their astrological birth sign can be original and appropriate (see Star Chart, page 89), but you can also have a lot of fun with Chinese birth signs, a highly complex system of divination that is at least three thousand years old. Legend has it that Buddha invited all the animals to a new year celebration, but only twelve turned up. Because of their loyalty, he decided to name a year after each of them and decreed that any human born within that animal's year would take on its characteristics, both good and bad. To determine the right sign, you need to find out the year, month and, in some cases, date of birth of the person for whom you wish to choose a gift.*

1900 Jan 31 - Feb 18 1901
1912 Feb 18 - Feb 5 1913
1924 Feb 5 - Jan 23 1925
1936 Jan 24 - Feb 10 1937
1948 Feb 10 - Jan 28 1949
1960 Jan 28 - Feb 14 1961
1972 Jan 15 - Feb 2 1973
1984 Feb 2 - Feb 19 1985
1996 Feb 19 - Feb 6 1997

◀ THE RAT is the sign of charm. A person born under this sign makes friends easily, is impulsive and adventurous (a **parachute or bungee jump**), intelligent and sharp-minded. They can also be greedy, bad-tempered, aggressive and terrible at handling financial affairs. Above all, the Rat loves money, food and socializing and tends to be over-ambitious. **A meal at the classiest restaurant in town, a magnum of champagne or a hamper full of delicacies** will all appeal to the gourmet Rat.

1901 Feb 19 - Feb 7 1902
1913 Feb 6 - Feb 25 1914
1925 Jan 24 - Feb 12 1926
1937 Feb 11 - Jan 30 1938
1949 Jan 29 - Feb 16 1950
1961 Feb 15 - Feb 4 1962
1973 Feb 3 - Jan 22 1974
1985 Feb 20 - Feb 8 1986
1997 Feb 7 - Jan 27 1998

▲ THE OX is a worker and knows that prosperity will only come through fortitude and hard graft. The patient Ox loves order and tradition and tends to be a stubborn stick-in-the-mud when it comes to new ideas. Never give the phlegmatic Ox anything that is frivolous or newfangled; only practical and long-lasting gifts will appeal. The office Ox will appreciate a sturdy **old-fashioned fountain pen** (the kind you fill up from a bottle of ink, not cartridges) and a **leather-bound blotter pad**.

▶ THE TIGER is the sign of courage. Tigers are powerful, passionate, daring and demand respect. They love any gift that requires them to perform and be the centre of attention. **Colourful juggling balls** would go down well with this dynamic personality. Tigers care little for materialistic responsibilities such as paying the rent. They are impulsive and indecisive and love faddish and fun items. A **jar of brightly-coloured fizzing sweets**, a **zany computer game** or **clothes in the latest fashion** are the perfect (attention-grabbing) present for this lover of life.

1902 Feb 8 - Jan 28 1903
1914 Jan 26 - Feb 13 1915
1926 Feb 13 - Feb 1 1927
1938 Jan 31 - Feb 18 1939
1950 Feb 17 - Feb 5 1951
1962 Feb 5 - Jan 24 1963
1974 Jan 23 - Feb 10 1975
1986 Feb 9 - Jan 28 1987
1998 Jan 28 - Feb 15 1999

1903 Jan 29 - Feb 15 1904
1915 Feb 14 - Feb 2 1916
1927 Feb 2 - Jan 22 1928
1939 Feb 19 - Feb 7 1940
1951 Feb 6 - Feb 26 1952
1963 Jan 25 - Feb 12 1964
1975 Feb 11 - Jan 30 1976
1987 Jan 29 - Feb 16 1988
1999 Feb 16 - Feb 4 2000

◀ THE HARE is the sign of virtue. Hares are graceful, sensuous, sensitive, diplomatic and well-balanced. They are self-assured and know exactly what they like to eat, do and buy. They are good at saving money and also spending it on the good things in life. An **all-expenses-paid day at a health farm** or a **visit to a beauty parlour** are perfect Hare presents. Ever the conformist, the Hare would appreciate some tasteful **silk boxer shorts**, a **cashmere sweater** or a **case of fine wine.**

▶ THE DRAGON is the sign of luck. The Dragon possesses charisma and is strong-willed, magnanimous, bursting with vitality and thrives on challenge. A **mind-stretching puzzle** will amuse and alert this most self-confident of people. The Dragon would probably appreciate a **portrait or photograph** (of him- or herself). Other traits include perfection and efficiency: a Dragon would love **five identical, new shirts**, so they can avoid having to make the tedious decision of what to put on in the morning.

1904 Feb 16 - Feb 3 1905
1916 Feb 3 - Jan 22 1917
1928 Jan 23 - Feb 9 1929
1940 Feb 8 - Jan 26 1941
1952 Feb 27 - Feb 13 1953
1964 Feb 13 - Feb 1 1965
1976 Jan 31 - Feb 17 1977
1988 Feb 17 - Feb 5 1989

▶The Sheep is the sign of art. The Sheep is an instigator of peace and harmony, a connoisseur of culture and literature and a lover of luxury. Never forget birthdays, anniversaries or special occasions as this would hurt this sensitive lamb. The fastidious Sheep is a stickler for hygiene so **scented soaps and oils** and **pastel-coloured bath salts** will make them bleat. Ever the caring soul, win their approval by **donating to a charity for children or animals.**

1907 Feb 13 - Feb 1 1908
1919 Feb 1 - Feb 19 1920
1931 Feb 17 - Feb 5 1932
1943 Feb 5 - Jan 24 1944
1955 Jan 24 - Feb 11 1956
1967 Feb 8 - Jan 29 1968
1979 Jan 28 - Feb 15 1980
1991 Feb 15 - Feb 3 1992

▶The Rooster is the sign of candour. Aggressive, self-assured heroes, Roosters are proud of their fine feathers and impeccable carriage. Accessories, such as **precisely designed earrings, apposite tiepins or monogrammed leather** are perfect tokens for these princely fowls. Ever the knight in shining armour, this brave fowl will (if their feathers are ruffled) enter into battle with military precision; winning fights is high on the Rooster agenda.

1909 Jan 22 - Feb 9 1910
1921 Feb 8 - Jan 27 1922
1933 Jan 26 - Feb 13 1934
1945 Feb 13 - Feb 1 1946
1957 Jan 31 - Feb 17 1958
1969 Feb 17 - Feb 5 1970
1981 Feb 5 - Jan 24 1982
1993 Jan 23 - Feb 9 1994

1906 Jan 25 - Feb 12 1907
1918 Feb 11 - Jan 31 1919
1930 Jan 30 - Feb 16 1931
1942 Feb 15 - Feb 4 1943
1954 Feb 3 - Jan 23 1955
1966 Jan 21 - Feb 8 1967
1978 Feb 7 - Jan 27 1979
1990 Jan 27 - Feb 14 1991

▲The Horse is the sign of elegance and ardour. A Horse is cheerful, popular, perceptive, talkative and quick-witted. However, they can also be hot-tempered and unpredictable - what they love with a passion could be in their hit list a few days later. Any gift given to this character should appeal to their vivacious, energetic and impetuous side. A **brightly coloured tie** or **waistcoat** will appeal to this showy dresser. Timekeeping is not a strong point, so a pocket computer or fashion watch would keep them bang on schedule.

1911 Jan 30 - Feb 17 1912
1923 Feb 16 - Feb 4 1924
1935 Feb 4 - Jan 23 1936
1947 Jan 22 - Feb 9 1948
1959 Feb 8 - Jan 27 1960
1971 Jan 27 - Feb 14 1972
1983 Feb 13 - Feb 1 1984
1995 Jan 31 - Feb 18 1996

▲The Pig is the sign of honesty. The easy-going, kind and understanding Pig possesses the warmest heart of all the signs. They gain great joy from the simplest tokens - **a big chocolate heart** or a **gold heart-shaped locket** would bring a tear to their little eye. They are terrific socializers and love joining in anything. **Membership of a suitable club or association** would thrill them. Being generous and willing to please, their greatest fault is the inability to say "No". Whether it is to another piece of chocolate cake or a request for assistance from a stranger, they just can't help over-indulging, to the detriment of themselves. Help by making **a big sign with the bold word "NO"** to sit on their desk.

▶The Monkey is the sign of fantasy and invention. They are good improvisers, quick-witted, clever and capable of drawing a crowd with their inimitable guile and charm. The Monkey loves to please and perform. Challenge this agile mind with a **pack of cards and a box of conjuring tricks**. Monkeys have a natural ability to pick up a new language or dialect; put that mimicking ability to the test with a **language course or tape**. They are also especially vain about their hair. Top-class **grooming products,** or a **cut and blow dry**, are winning presents for this highly coiffured individual.

1908 Feb 2 - Jan 21 1909
1920 Feb 20 - Feb 7 1921
1932 Feb 6 - Jan 25 1933
1944 Jan 25 - Feb 12 1945
1956 Feb 12 - Jan 30 1957
1968 Jan 30 - Feb 16 1969
1980 Feb 16 - Feb 4 1981
1992 Feb 4 - Jan 22 1993

1910 Feb 10 - Jan 29 1911
1922 Jan 28 - Feb 15 1923
1934 Feb 14 - Feb 3 1935
1946 Feb 2 - Jan 21 1947
1958 Feb 18 - Feb 7 1959
1970 Feb 6 - Jan 26 1971
1982 Jan 25 - Feb 12 1983
1994 Feb 10 - Jan 30 1995

◀The Dog is the sign of idealism and loyalty. If you're in trouble, forget S-O-S, just dial D-O-G and they'll come running. Dogs are faithful, reliable, selfless, compassionate and protective towards their friends. Kind thoughts and acts of good faith are gratefully appreciated by this playful pooch. A **surprise birthday cake** or **carefully planned outing** both rate highly on the 'woof, woof, wag' scale.

1905 Feb 4 - Jan 24 1906
1917 Jan 23 - Feb 10 1918
1929 Feb 10 - Jan 29 1930
1941 Jan 27 - Feb 14 1942
1953 Feb 14 - Feb 2 1954
1965 Feb 2 - Jan 20 1966
1977 Feb 18 - Feb 6 1978
1989 Feb 6 - Jan 26 1990

◀The Snake is the sign of wisdom. The intuitive, mystically inclined Snake loves using charm to get what they want from life. This ambitious person always loves to receive **expensive intoxicating scent** or **beautiful jewellery** (gold cuff-links and real gems, not junk sparklers) to promote their favourite pastime of winning hearts and enticing compliments.

There are very few events in this world that are as emotive as a wedding. Even the most hard-nosed cynics have been reduced to feeling something close to sentimental during this ceremony. Centre stage on this momentous occasion is the loving couple, who have slaved for months over the endless preparations and battled through hours of tiresome family squabbles to reach this moment of vow-exchanging solemnity.

In spite of the preceding dramas, all are agreed that it has been worthwhile. Each of the exhausted individuals has gained a lifetime partner, to be at their side through thick and thin. Fantastic though this is, it is the gifts that are really the pay-off at the end of the long road to getting hitched.

Matrimony is a key gift-giving occasion, ranking right up there alongside Christmas and birthdays. If someone you know is getting married and especially if you are attending the wedding, it is customary, if not compulsory, to give some kind of token. From best friend to casual acquaintance, there's a gift out there just begging to be given.

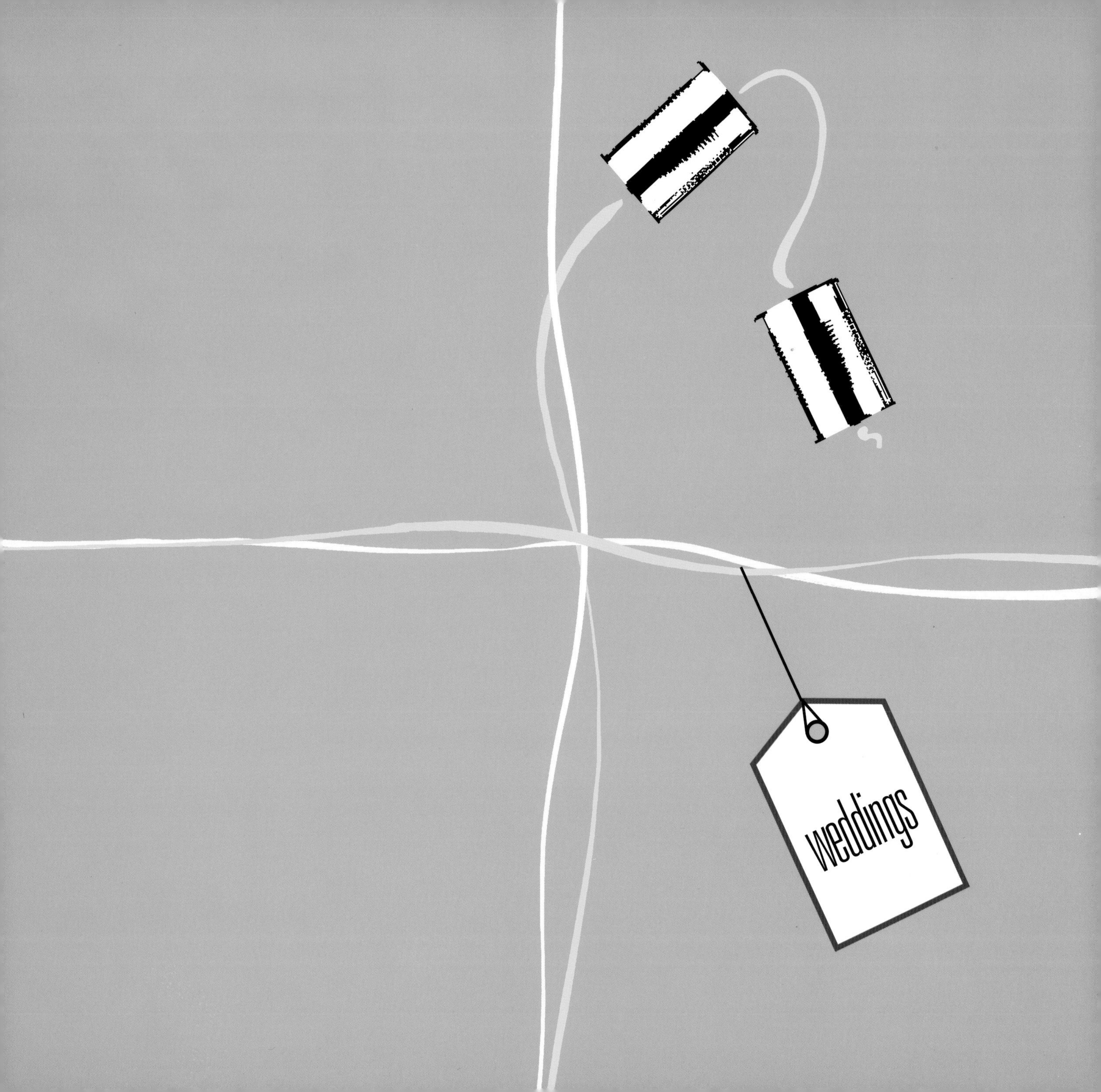
weddings

Give the bride-to-be ***a rubber stamp of her married name and pen,*** *with which she can practise signing her new title.*

engagement

TRADITIONALLY, *an engagement is the time for a couple and their respective families to prepare for the wedding. Being engaged is not only the period during which you need to make quite sure that life is the sentence you want to spend with your intended, but also a time when you can justifiably bask in the limelight, be the centre of attention and also be thoroughly spoilt by all and sundry.*

HAS YOUR best friend, who's been kissing frogs for so long, finally found Prince Charming who will whisk her away to live happily ever after? If so, why not find her a gift that is in tune with the fairytale quality of the occasion? A pair of **antique slippers** or shoes, found in a flea market or antique costume shop, will symbolise Cinderella finding her prince and at the same time mark the giant step she is taking.

"HI, I'm not in to take your call, so please speak after the squeak"... Squeeeaaakk! "Sarah, it's me. I can't believe you're going to be Mrs Redding. Congratulations"... Beeep. "Hello, Sarah, it's Aunt Julia. Darling, such wonderful news. We must celebrate"... Beeep. "Slobby. How did you manage to keep this a secret for so long? I can't *believe* you didn't tell me. It's fantastic!"... Beeep. "Hi, it's Will. I never thought you'd make it before me. Who's going to be my surrogate date now? Larry is a lucky guy"... Beeep. 30 messages later, Sarah is reeling from all the kind and caring words of good luck and advice from her friends and family around the world. She is also stunned that they all called on the same day. What a coincidence. But no - little does Sarah know that you spent last week on the phone, asking everyone to ring her on the same day, thereby automatically compiling **a tape recording of all the messages** as a souvenir of her time as the novice Mrs Redding.❤

AFTER ALL these years, they have finally decided to tie the knot. You all hoped it would happen and now that it has you want to be amongst the first to congratulate them on their engagement, in an original way. So does everybody else. As a matter of fact, you have been unable to get through on the telephone, as the whole world and his wife is attempting to do exactly the same. Forget the phone and pick up the video camera. Film your message of good luck and felicitations, along with those of your mutual friends and give them the complete **congratulatory video compilation** as a gift.❤

DON'T TELL us you haven't practised writing a signature, the one that you would take on marrying a particular sweetheart. Of course you have! Therefore your girlfriend's engagement gift of **a rubber stamp of your new married name, a pen and writing pad** with which to practise signing the new title is most apt if not entirely necessary as, like most of us, you are probably able to do it in your sleep by the time you have accepted his proposal of marriage.

COLLABORATION, co-ordination and co-operation are the key words here. Ask friends and family of the bride and groom-to-be to donate photographs of the couple before they knew each other. Once you have collected a substantial number, **create a collage** and frame it. This will make a fascinating piece of future nostalgia and it hardly costs a thing.❤

JEWELLERY is the classic present for either of the betrothed couple to give the other to mark their engagement. Rather than buying a ready-made item and risk giving something that is not to the other's taste, a thoughtful gift, which also emphasises your longterm intentions, would be **an uncut gem,** to be treasured and made up on your first wedding anniversary into a pendant, an eternity ring, a tiepin or even the tip of a pen.

best friend

Your best friend *is getting married - what amazing news! The wedding of a dear friend is certainly cause for a major celebration. After all, it's not every day that your soulmate, the one who knows your innermost secrets (and vice versa), decides to take the matrimonial plunge. And naturally, being the most important person in their lives (apart from their intended), you want to reflect this top-drawer position with a wedding gift of the utmost consideration.*

The longer it takes a couple to make up their minds to take the plunge, the more ecstatic are the friends who have been pushing and teasing for what seems like forever. They feel that it was an almost Olympian achievement to get to this point and this needs to be rewarded. Get all their friends to club together, then unveil **a sporting trophy or medal**, engraved with everyone's signature and a plaque saying: "Well done! This decision was undertaken in the record time of 3 years, 2 months and 21 days."❤

To appear on the cover of a gossip magazine is a matter of course for a superstar who has become engaged, whereas for us mere mortals a mention in the classified section is as close as we will probably get to our fifteen minutes of fame. Unless, of course, a dear friend has the initiative and time to make **a framed mock-up of a magazine cover**, with a superimposed photograph of the happy couple gazing ecstatically from beneath the title of the magazine in question.

Your friend has finally got engaged, but still hasn't set a date for the big day. Will they really go ahead and tie the knot or is this just another empty promise? Friends can show their support for a couple's prospective union through presents that are suggestive rather than expensive. **A book on nautical knots** might be a not-so-subtle hint of encouragement towards their forthcoming exchange of vows.❤

Following the symbolic theme, the gift of 'a pair' of anything will delight the newly engaged couple. To enhance their enjoyment of the many congratulatory bottles of champagne they will be given, scour the markets to find them a pair of **crystal champagne flutes** and present them in a beautiful box with a starter bottle of vintage champagne.

As soon as the news gets out their doorbells will be ringing non-stop as bunches of congratulatory flowers are delivered. Make sure your **floral tribute** has some extra meaning:

Tulip - the Persian symbol of perfect love
Forget-me-not - true love
Ivy-leafed Geranium - bridal favour
Phlox - we are united
Pink - purity of affection
Water Lily - purity of heart
Wood Sorrel - joy
Ivy - friendship, immortality and a symbolic attachment.

secrets

They know you know. You were there together, for heaven's sake. Moreover, you have endless photographic evidence of the wild days spent together in your youth. Remember the occasion in Southern Spain when you, er...? Yup. The photos are still tucked away in your underwear drawer. Do you recollect that naked midnight streak down the main street? Of course, you found *those* incriminating pictures only last week. And what about the six previous lovers your best friend conveniently omitted to mention to their prospective spouse? No problem. You have charming portraits of them all in various romantic poses with your partner in crime. We all have skeletons in the cupboard and if you hold the evidence of times and people best forgotten, a wedding present which will greatly relieve your friend is **a beautiful antique box** which, when opened, will be found to be **filled with shredded photographs** of 'you-know-who' and 'remember when'.

Is it written in the stars or is it not? Is it a match made in heaven or hell? Find out by giving the blissful couple **an astrological compatibility chart**. You know the date, time of birth and location of your best friend's entry into this world. You just need to discover the relevant details of their betrothed in order to commission an astrological insight into their union. (Hint: if the outcome is an intimation of unmitigated disaster, think very carefully before presenting the chart!)

A present which will relieve your friend is ***a beautiful antique box filled with shredded photographs*** *of you-know-who and remember - when.*

the special day

In western tradition, even when your best friend of all time is getting hitched, it is expected that you should give a gift directed at the couple. But in the East this would be thought of as a strange and impersonal gesture. Instead, a gift given to your most favoured friend would be both intimate and valuable, to symbolise the value of your friendship. **Jewellery** is always a hot favourite. Why not find something which includes their **birthstone** (see *Star Chart, page 89*) or a **bracelet of lucky charms** that can be added to on each anniversary.❤

Hopefully, your best friend and their future husband or wife share a common interest. Scour the antiquarian book shops for **a beautifully bound first edition**, thereby finding a gift which will interest them at the time but also increase in value (like their love) with the passing years.

Whether beauty is in the eye of the beholder or love is blind, *you* might never figure out what he sees in her or she in him. But does it really matter if you don't find them attractive? Of course not. Commission **a portrait or photograph** of the happy couple, so the shine in their eyes when they were newly, madly and deeply in love can be captured for posterity. Who knows, if you choose the right artist it might also be worth something one day.❤

Oh yes, we all love having best friends, but when that friendship brings with it the task of being their best man one might feel a tinge of regret. With this 'honour' comes the chore of having to give an embarrassing speech and the search for that extra special present. Think well in advance, dig out that underused camcorder and **produce a video of the couple's life** to premiere on a big screen at the reception. This will not only solve both the aforementioned problems, but will also earn you some genuine applause. (Hint: you will need to film some of their favourite places, interview their friends, sneak some footage of the unsuspecting twosome, then edit your masterpiece with an appropriately tongue-in-cheek voiceover.)❤

One's wedding day passes at the speed of light. One minute you're exchanging vows and the next you're en route to your honeymoon destination. The in-between bits are a blur. Never mind, in a couple of weeks, the home video and nuptial portraits will jog your blurred memories. But why wait that long? An inspired friend has had the foresight to **take Polaroid photographs**, giving you **the pictures *and* the camera** as a present as you depart in your going-away outfits.❤

The wedding night. Now here is a much joked-about subject. As their best friend, ensuring that the least they get is a good night's sleep (what else?), would seem to be a helpful gesture. Fill the twilight zone between leaving the wedding and taking off on honeymoon by giving them **the keys to a fabulous, pre-paid hotel room** where they can recharge their batteries before departing to the destination of their dreams. (Hint: this is a gift that needs advance planning and the co-operation of the couple.)

•When *Viscount Linley* married the lovely Serena Stanhope, one of their more unusual gifts was a bread bin. Dull and unoriginal? Not in this case, for inside was a loaf of *Mother's Pride* bread and a cheeky note proclaiming "The perfect breakfast for the morning after!"❤

However wonderful the wedding day has been, every bride will tell you that it went by too quickly. By the time she has wiped away a tear, whispered "I do", said "Hi, Aunt Mary", "Thanks for coming, cousin Pat" and chucked her bouquet in the air, it is all over. If you are lucky enough to lay your hands on her wedding bouquet, there are a lot better things to do with it than let it wither away in a vase. Frame the previously **pressed petals in the shape of a heart** and transform it into a memento to treasure - after all, you are her best friend.❤

If you catch the wedding bouquet, give it to the bride as a memento by framing the ***pressed petals into the shape of a heart.*** ❤

a family wedding

When a member of the family gets married, the purchasing of the perfect present should be a straightforward affair. In fact, with the same blood coursing through your veins, it should be a piece of wedding cake. You love them, grew up with them, know them inside out. That may be so, but family ties also extend to that cousin you haven't seen since you played Mummys and Daddys together at the age of three or the spinster aunt you have so diligently avoided for the past ten years. They need gifts and you need help in coming up with the ideas!

A wedding day needs not only to be fun, but also to be remembered as such. A professional photographer will be busy following the bride and groom, but will have difficulty in capturing the more spontaneous, behind-the-scenes action. The happy couple, too, are usually oblivious to most of the goings-on, either because they are too busy or too tipsy. Give every guest **a disposable camera** when they arrive, collect it when they leave and, when they return from honeymoon, present the newlyweds with an album replete with impromptu photographs of their friends and family as a lasting reminder of a really happy day.

As a member of the family, give something that is both a tribute to the newlyweds and can be handed down. A **stained glass window** or **a windowpane etched with the couple's initials or a sketch of their house** will last a lifetime and beyond.

Capture the behind-the-scenes action of a wedding by giving every guest ***a disposable camera*** *when they arrive and collecting it as they leave.*

wedding traditions

At a family *wedding more than at any marital occasion, it's so important to do exactly the right thing, to play it by the book. Many wedding customs and superstitions are plain old poppycock, but you can be sure that someone in the family will take them seriously. So here are a few do's and taboos to help you along the way.*

ANTIQUE LINEN, crisp new linen, bed linen, initialled linen, linen napkins and linen tablecloths are all sought-after items in the materialistic portfolios of the engaged couple. They are gifts that will be appreciated, but can be left to those unbound by genetic ties. On the other hand, a **pillowcase filled with coins** collected since they announced their engagement is a practical but personal gift, one that would only be acceptable if given by a family member.

MARRIAGE is about family, about continuity. This is a theme that lends itself well to present giving, as opposed to present buying. **Passing things on** will ensure that they remain in the family and will eventually age into antiques. Choose an object with a meaning or story attached, maybe even something that has already been passed down to you.

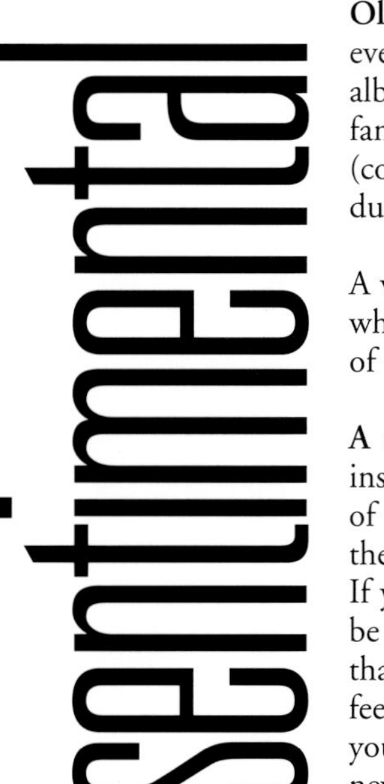

FAMILY TO FAMILY

The custom of the bride's family giving a dowry to the groom's family has all but died out in the western world. However, it is still a customary goodwill gesture for the families to exchange tokens, so here are some suggestions:

Old family photos, or even a complete family album with names and family history attached (could save all that introducing on the day).

A **whisky decanter**, from which to toast the union of the two families.

A small silver bowl, inscribed with the names of the two families and the date of the marriage. If you don't want to be so serious, anything that has a sentimental feel about it will win you a smile from your new family.

BRIDESMAIDS

If you are going to play it by the wedding etiquette book, then remember the gifts for the bridesmaids (and especially if she or they are the bride's sister and best friend). This task is the duty of the groom. You can't go wrong with a piece of antique jewellery such as a locket or (friendship) bracelet, but what better than a **fine gold chain**, the links symbolising the bands of communication and marriage.

MOTHER TO DAUGHTER

The making of **a decorative quilt** has been a custom in the United States since colonial times. The women in an area would sit with the bride's mother to create this work of art for the wedding bed. Short of starting your own sewing circle, this project would be a little ambitious to undertake, but with the thought in mind you could enlist the help of an expert seamstress to design and make a quilt, or visit an antique textile specialist to find a beautiful old example. (Hint: involve your daughter in this gift to ensure the result is to her taste.)

ANOTHER tradition that has passed into history along with dowries is '**the bottom drawer**'. Each year of her daughter's life the bride's mother would put aside a little something for the day when her daughter married and moved to her own home. These would normally be items such as beautiful lace, linen, fine embroidered tablecloths and napkins, maybe her own wedding dress and other precious family trinkets; all stored, as the name suggests, in the bottom drawer. Why not recreate this tradition by buying and filling an old wooden blanket chest with a set of **monogrammed towels** or **a beautiful antique tablecloth or bedspread**. Alternatively, buy them **a chest of drawers** and really fill the bottom drawer.

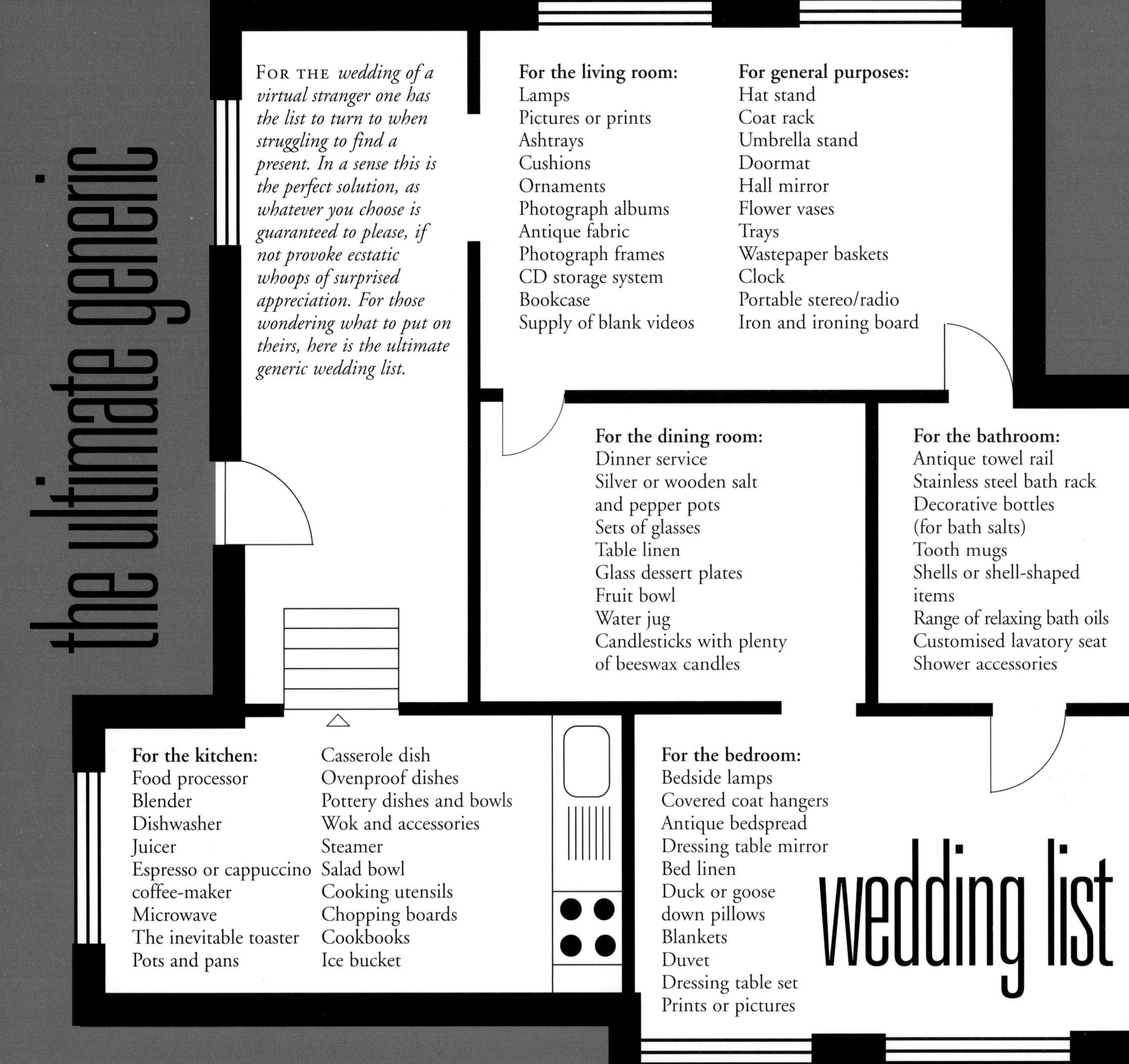

the ultimate generic wedding list

For the wedding of a virtual stranger one has the list to turn to when struggling to find a present. In a sense this is the perfect solution, as whatever you choose is guaranteed to please, if not provoke ecstatic whoops of surprised appreciation. For those wondering what to put on theirs, here is the ultimate generic wedding list.

For the living room:
Lamps
Pictures or prints
Ashtrays
Cushions
Ornaments
Photograph albums
Antique fabric
Photograph frames
CD storage system
Bookcase
Supply of blank videos

For general purposes:
Hat stand
Coat rack
Umbrella stand
Doormat
Hall mirror
Flower vases
Trays
Wastepaper baskets
Clock
Portable stereo/radio
Iron and ironing board

For the dining room:
Dinner service
Silver or wooden salt and pepper pots
Sets of glasses
Table linen
Glass dessert plates
Fruit bowl
Water jug
Candlesticks with plenty of beeswax candles

For the bathroom:
Antique towel rail
Stainless steel bath rack
Decorative bottles (for bath salts)
Tooth mugs
Shells or shell-shaped items
Range of relaxing bath oils
Customised lavatory seat
Shower accessories

For the kitchen:
Food processor
Blender
Dishwasher
Juicer
Espresso or cappuccino coffee-maker
Microwave
The inevitable toaster
Pots and pans
Casserole dish
Ovenproof dishes
Pottery dishes and bowls
Wok and accessories
Steamer
Salad bowl
Cooking utensils
Chopping boards
Cookbooks
Ice bucket

For the bedroom:
Bedside lamps
Covered coat hangers
Antique bedspread
Dressing table mirror
Bed linen
Duck or goose down pillows
Blankets
Duvet
Dressing table set
Prints or pictures

symbolic

They're more than just acquaintances, but not amongst your closest friends. Even so, you don't want to appear so unimaginative that you have to refer to the list. Or maybe they haven't a list and you've wracked your brains unsuccessfully for a gift they'll use and enjoy. If you're having trouble finding a token to mark the occasion, perhaps one of the following symbols will inspire you:

Long life -The aim of all marriages is to last, for better or for worse, for richer, for poorer, through sickness and health till death us do part. The reality of those words seems impossible to imagine at this stage; it is as much as you can do to battle your way through the wedding preparations - let alone plan the rest of your lives together. However, with the hope of a lifetime together ahead of them, the perfect gift for every couple is a **symbol of longevity** to see them through.

The circle is a universal symbol for the wholeness of life, a form that has no beginning and no end. Twin circles, according to Dante, represent love and knowledge and overlapping circles are an ancient Christian symbol, hence the tradition of a wedding ring comprising one or more continuous circles. Why not use this common geometric form to devise a gift with real symbolic meaning. Circular table mats and coasters, a circular Chinese rug, a circular wedding wreath made with appropriate flowers, are all possibilities. If the couple's ethnic origins are different a unique spherical present would be an antique globe.

The thistle, as an emblem of Scotland, is also a traditional symbol of longevity. The ultimate gift here would be a weekend break in Scotland but, failing that, a box of Scottish shortbread or other Scottish speciality bearing the thistle motif would be, well, not so exciting, but certainly a little easier to organise.

The turtle is an animal that symbolises longevity. To catch sight of a turtle laying its eggs is supposed to be very lucky. If your pocket doesn't quite stretch to the flamboyant gesture of an all-expenses-paid sun-drenched holiday to a beach where this rare event will take place, then take a slightly cheaper option, and adopt a turtle at the local zoo for the courting couple. Alternatively, go for a turtle-shaped doorstop or paperweight, or even a tin of **'mock turtle' soup**.

The hare is also a symbol of longevity. Take the engagees to a night at a dog track, where traditionally a hare was used to entice the greyhounds to run faster. They may only clap eyes on a mechanical hare, but a good time will be enjoyed by all.

The bells - A string to hang by the door, an antique doorbell for their new home, windchimes for their garden, are gifts which will symbolise their continuing happiness.

The butterfly - It wouldn't be eco-friendly to give a living example, but a hunt around the antique shops might prove successful in finding a framed butterfly or an article of jewellery in the right shape.

hen party & stag night

It's incredible to think that this time tomorrow she will be married. Though it is obviously very exciting, there is always a touch of sadness as she moves on to the next stage of her life. Her days of wolf whistling at the sight of hunky men are nearly over. Just twenty-four hours left in which to let rip. Her final day of freedom must be placed in the hands of her friends, whose duty it is to lead her astray and keep her nervous mind off the day ahead. Self-indulgence and over-indulgence are paramount. However, make sure she is in the arms of her teddy bear before the witching hour; she won't thank you if she looks a wreck on her wedding day.

Organising a **hen party** is almost as much fun as being at one. The trick is to find some entertainment that is really new and hot. The locality should be your first concern as that dictates all else, and an activity is always better than just hanging out at the local bar. Karaoke is an old favourite (but not a good choice for a power lady). However, if she falls into the achiever or affiliation category, some kind of exhilarating fun such as **go-carting or a night at the races** would be perfect choices and would appeal to both. To avoid embarrassment, all discussion of payment should be settled between her friends at the time of invitation rather than at the end of the party.

Just like the old saying 'You can never be too rich or too thin' - a budding bride can never have too many sets of **lingerie**. Slipping into a pair of silk cammies or lounging around in a lace teddy will not only get her heart racing around the honeymoon suite. Remember that shops will rarely let you exchange underwear, so make sure you know her size, and please, girls, don't be vulgar, they'll only end up in the bin.

If it is your sister or a childhood friend that is getting married, then spend the day **doing something reminiscent of your youth**. This might be a nostalgic trip to the garden shed where you played doctors and nurses or to the ice-rink where you showed off to the local talent.

The build-up to the big day has taken its toll on your best friend. Instead of glowing with happiness she resembles an anaemic toad that has just crawled out from under a stone. Heaven forbid that she should turn up at the altar in this state. What she needs is **a complete day in the beauty salon** with every pampering treatment laid on.

Firm favourite *for a groom's single send off is still* ***the stag night****. The very words conjure up images of staggering figures, horrific schoolboy pranks and grown men weeping like babies. The likelihood of some kind of bad behaviour taking place in the name of fun is almost certain and will largely depend on the best man's interpretation of a fun stag rave-up. For resting on his undependable shoulders is the responsibility for initiating and organising the last day single of his so-called best friend. Ring! Ring! calling all best men! - please note it's not every person's idea of fun to be strapped to a lamp-post, stripped naked and left stranded in the local high street or deposited dead drunk with a leg in plaster on an overnight train to Timbuktu. On the other hand, some fellas would cringe at the very thought of a quiet intimate dinner with a few old chums without even the hint of a leggy chick jumping out of a cake. When it comes to the subject of gift giving, don't bother giving it a second thought, as this task once again falls on the shoulders of the best man.*

❤ **The Affianced Affiliation Stag Party:** The friendly, aims-to-please affiliation groom will not want to make any waves with his future bride. However, being of a sociable, clubbable nature he'll go along quite happily with whatever's put on his plate. If he's given the choice for his preferred evening's excitement, don't expect a conclusive reply. Whatever you want will be fine by him; so long as everyone else enjoys the evening he'll have a ball, so absolutely anything goes. Gifts for the friendly affiliated male: Old school or sport's team **photo** - framed and signed, if possible, by those in the picture. **A membership** to a sporting or members' club - he'll want to belong. So they can keep fit together: a **bicycle made for two.** A **hip flask** and a **nest of glasses** - to warm the cockles when out on those hearty country walks. While he would absolutely cringe at the sight of himself immortalised on canvas, he may well appreciate a **portrait of his fiancée.** For the long summer evenings' entertaining: **a barbecue set** complete with chef's hat and apron. A pair of **new shoes, signed on the soles** by all his friends. When he kneels down the whole church will see what a smashing fella he is! **Cuff-links engraved** with his and her initials intertwined. A **portable CD player** with **two pairs of headphones.** The key to every woman's heart is a man who accepts his fair share of domestic duties. Supply him with the ultimate household cleaning accessory - a pair of **rubber gloves and an apron** (although a dishwasher would go down better).

The Accredited Achievement Stag Party: The competitive, ambitious achiever will want to preserve this night on record for all time as the party that ended all parties. The most expensive champagne, the swankiest venue and the greatest number of alcoholic casualties are the required criteria for his perfect event. Showing off his nifty footwork at a celebrity-studded nightspot, dining on the finest in a private room at an exclusive members' club or an overnight trip to some famous foreign location (Paris, Monte Carlo, Las Vegas) would all be perfect stag night send offs. The key phrase to remember here is 'make it the best evening money can buy'.

Gifts for the over-achieving man: A pair of **showy cuff-links**, the bigger and crustier the better. A state-of-the-art **watch** to ensure he definitely makes it to the church on time. **A pass to the VIP lounge** at the airport. Commission a **portrait or photograph** of the groom in his favourite designer suit or state-of-the-art sportswear. **A mountain bike**, top-of-the-range of course, and all the right gear to wear while riding it. The latest **prizewinning books** for a little light honeymoon reading. The biggest and most gadget-packed **Swiss army knife.** A **Mont Blanc** pen with which to sign the marriage register.

♛ **The Positive Power Stag Party:** This dominant, decisive groom will have a very good idea of exactly how he wants to spent the evening, so take your orders from him or risk your friendship. If this information is not forthcoming and as a friend you think you know his likes and dislikes, go ahead, but remember to keep it to the minimum of fuss. Gifts for the man who has everything: You'll already know where his honeymoon destination is, so supply him with everything he'll ever need to know about it with a **top-of-the-range travel guide.** Even a simple marital activity such as a walk in the country would not be complete for this dominant individual without a **compass and a commando survival book.** No-one is likely to forget that he's in charge, but maybe a little something to emphasise his superior role in the relationship, such as **monogrammed slippers, shirts or dressing gown.** For the power golfer a graphite **Big Bertha No.1 wood.** A pair of **understated but obviously expensive cuff-links** (Note: no sentimental engraving.) Arrange for a **huge bouquet of flowers to be sent to his new wife** (on his behalf) when they get back from their honeymoon.

Throughout our lives we are faced with challenges that have to be met and mastered if we are to evolve in tune with the world. From birth, we proceed to an affirmation of religious beliefs, followed by the inevitable teenage blues. Adolescence over and done with, graduation looms between us and adulthood. Then there's that first job and with an income comes independence.

The successful opening of each new door in life is a turning point and should be recognised by others in the form of congratulations, celebrations or commiserations. Presents are the natural way of marking our journey through life.

When searching for the ideal gift, there are two routes to take. The first is to give something that represents the achievement, enabling the receiver to look back with pride. The second is to give something that facilitates the rise to the next level. Whichever of these you follow, your gift will provide a little extra encouragement and motivation in the recipient's quest for power, position, achievement and the ultimate goal of self-fulfilment.

a new
chapter in life

For a girl, an item of jewellery is always a popular birth or christening present. Find out the child's **birthstone** (*see Star Chart, page 89*) and buy or have made a tiny pendant, locket or bracelet set with the appropriate stone.❤

When a child is born, you will want to wish them a safe journey through life. A **charm of St Christopher**, the patron saint of travellers, will form the beginning of a charm bracelet which can be added to on each birthday.❤

Even though most babies are born with little or no hair to speak of, there will come a day when there is a healthy head of hair that needs grooming. A **baby's hair-brush set** is a practical gift and, later on, can be used by the child to keep his/her teddies and dolls smartly turned out.

The stork is a universal symbol of childbirth. In Greek mythology the stork was the bringer and nourisher of life, longevity and happiness. Why not give that bonnie babe a **little china stork** to watch over him/her while sleeping.❤

The oak tree has long been a symbol of strength and hospitality. Planting **an oak tree** to honour the birth of a child is more than a symbol of long life. The growth of the tall, spreading tree will enhance his or her understanding of their place in nature.❤

*Plant **an oak tree** as a symbol of long life with the birth of a baby.*

happy birthday

THE WAY *to a parent's heart is most definitely through their newborn child. She has spent nine arduous months carrying an increasingly large sack of potatoes up and down stairs, shopping and to bed. He has gone on numerous midnight mercy missions for strange food-stuffs to satisfy her insatiable cravings. The prize has finally arrived in the form of a gurgling bundle of soft flesh. Now it's your job to mark the occasion with, yes, you've guessed it, a suitable gift.*

FOR THE FIRST few years a child's world is confined to home and the occasional well wrapped-up visit out; a young bird in the wild, however, is off to foreign lands as soon as it can spread its wings. Give the fledgeling traveller a taste of those wide open spaces by **adopting a wild duck** on his or her behalf. At birth, the duckling is ringed and its progress tracked, then a postcard is sent to its 'parent' from everywhere it is subsequently found.❤

• **AS SOON as his wife, Donna, announced that she was pregnant, actor *Dan Ackroyd* was desperate to know the sex of the baby, but, when she discovered this vital piece of information he was away in New York filming. No problem! Donna contacted the city authorities and 'IT'S A GIRL' was immediately announced in neon lights** in New York's Times Square.❤

THE ARRIVAL of a new member of the family is an undeniable cause for celebration and, of course, photographs, photographs and yet more photographs are an absolute must. The little prodigy's every move must be recorded for the family album, to keep in that special pocket in the wallet and framed to sit in pride of place around the house. But what about the parents? In all this fuss about the new arrival, their feelings and state of mind at the time of the birth can be forgotten forever. Why not provide them with an eternal reminder in the form of **their own portrait** (with offspring if they so desire), framed and **engraved with names and dates**?❤

UNFORTUNATELY the newborn baby's clock is rarely tuned to that of its parents and many sleepless hours will be spent carrying the bright-eyed infant around in the dawn hours. In these early months anything coloured or sparkling which will hold their attention is a godsend to the somnolent parent, so give the newborn **a coloured string of bells** (representing happiness) to hang in the bedroom or **a crystal on a chain** to hang at the window. Crystals are supposed to have remarkable powers - you can find one appropriate to the baby's birthsign and its ability to refract all the colours of the rainbow around the room will keep baby and parent content for hours.

IT IS traditional, but expensive, to give silver to a newborn child. If you are poor but clever, you will know that most **antique silver objects** can be bought for a comparative song in relation to their contemporary counterparts. Find an appropriate little object, but make it more personal by having it **engraved with the baby's name or initials.** A well-known and otherwise expensive jeweller will do this for you, with the added advantage that they will wrap the present in their signature paper. As a result the proud parents will believe you have spent an absolute fortune at the jewellers in question.

"IT ALL WENT SO quickly" is a frequent moan of parents whose children have fled the nest. With this in mind, a thoughtful gift would be a **childhood time capsule**. The contents of this can be gathered throughout the years and can incorporate such things as their first lock of hair, first teeth, photographs, school reports and other mementoes. Initiate this collection with the gift of **a beautifully bound album** or **an antique box** in which to store the treasures.❤

it's a girl

naming ceremonies

THE NEXT STEP *on the staircase of life is the naming ceremony, an occasion on which the gifts given are significant. If you are a godparent or guardian, think carefully about why you were chosen and try to emulate this quality in your choice of present; if a member of the family, a symbolic gift might be appropriate.*

***Agatha Christie,* could afford to be generous. However, even she was probably not aware of her generosity when she gave her godson the royalties to one of her stories, especially as the story became *The Mousetrap,* the most successful play in the history of British theatre.**

TRADITIONAL offerings are all very well and good, but what if this baby's parents are more of a funky than frumpy variety and, to make life even more difficult for you, they're plumping for a **New Age naming ceremony** rather than a christening. Move over you traditionalists, this is no place for silver crockery, cutlery, storks or bowls. You're dealing with a hip chicklet here. Think organic! Make it, don't buy it. The eco-friendly thing to do, of course, is to **plant a tree**, alternatively a lovingly scripted and framed **poem or saying** or a **hand-strung bead necklace** would make perfect post-modern presents.

first steps

FIRST STEPS: It won't be long before baby starts crawling, toddling then walking. The gift of a well-crafted **child's chair** could suggest to the toddler that instead of being a real tearabout terror, he or she could be a little adult (occasionally) and copy Mummy and Daddy by sitting down. If there's a **coat of arms** lurking in the family, have it painstakingly painted on. Any Scottish connections? **Upholster the chair** in the appropriate tartan. Or, most simply and satisfyingly, **stencil their name** on to the chair with your own fair hand.

IF YOU are a close friend and the parents are interested in religion, you can't go wrong with the offering of a relevant **religious book**. This will be a gift that the child will want to keep forever, so make sure it's a beautifully bound copy with a personal message written inside.

FIRST HAIRCUT: Some babies are born with a full head of curls that can be coiffured at bath time into a perfect Elvis quiff, while others struggle for months cultivating just one tuft. The first haircut is a poignant moment, so supply the wherewithal to preserve those early locks for posterity: **a beautiful pair of scissors and a pretty box or antique glass bottle.**

silver spoon

IF THE child isn't fortunate enough to be born with one in its mouth then ensure that he/she will grow up with one - traditionally, a popular christening gift was a **silver spoon**; girls would be given a dozen teaspoons, while boys received a soup spoon. This custom has died out, but the spoon remains and can now be accompanied by its faithful old chums the **knife and fork**. (Hint: if you can't stretch to silver, then find an initialled set.)

IT IS UNLIKELY that you will be able to emulate dear Agatha, but what you could do is **invest** in a project or on the stock market and make the investment **in the name of the child**. If your choice is a wise one, by the time the child grows up, he or she may be sitting on a small fortune. For the less daring, **Premium or Savings Bonds** may well earn them a tidy income in years to come.

Flowers for children

Coreopsis - Always cheerful
Potentilla - Maternal affection
Periwinkle, Blue - Early friendship
Primrose - Early youth
Scilla, White - Sweet innocence
Stock - Lasting beauty
Verbena, White - Pure and guileless

Star Signs	Lucky Day	Flowers	Colours	Lucky Gems	Lucky Number
Aries Mar 21 - Apr 20	Tuesday	Wild Rose, Red Carnation, Thistle	Bright Green, Pink, Red, Yellow	Ruby, Bloodstone, Diamond	Seven
Taurus Apr 21 - May 20	Friday	Lily-of-the-Valley, Violet	Shades of Blues	Sapphire, Emerald, Turquoise	Six
Gemini May 21 - June 21	Wednesday	Snapdragon, Sweet Pea, Clover	White, Silver, Yellow	Agate, Jade, Diamond, Crystal	Five
Cancer June 22 - July 22	Monday	Poppy, Iris, Madonna Lily	Emerald - Green, White	Emerald, Moonstone, Pearls	Two
Leo July 23 - Aug 22	Sunday	Marigold, Sunflower	Gold, Yellow, Orange	Amber, Topaz, Tourmaline	Four
Virgo Aug 23 - Sept 22	Wednesday	Corn Flower, Orange Blosssom	Pale Blue, Gold, Yellow	Cornelian, Jade, Zircon, Diamond	Ten
Libra Sept 23 - Oct 22	Friday	Violet, White Rose	Blue, Violet	Opal, Red Coral	Eight
Scorpio Oct 23 - Nov 21	Tuesday	Chrysanthemum, Geranium	Red, Rusty-Brown	Ruby, Fire-Opal	Nine
Sagittarius Nov 22 - Dec 20	Thursday	Carnation, Pink, Dandelion	Orange, Purple	Turquoise, Sapphire, Amethyst	Four
Capricorn Dec 21 - Jan 19	Saturday	Nightshade, Ivy, Hibiscus	Black, Grey, Violet	Onyx, Jet, Black Pearl	Three
Aquarius Jan 20 - Feb 18	Saturday	Snowdrop, Foxglove,Wisteria	Electric Blue, Green	Zircon, Ruby, Garnet, Malachite	Two
Pisces Feb 19 - Mar 20	Thursday	Orchid	Purple, Mauve, Sea Green	Sapphire, Emerald, Amethyst, Coral	Six

Nelson

Marilyn

Elvis

Marlene

New stars are discovered every day. To become an official member of the cosmos, each requires a name and NASA has now made it possible to '**buy a star** and name it. As the universe represents eternity, there can be no more powerful gift than to award a newborn child with an ever-present force called after them as a constant pointer on their long journey through life.

newborn

star personality

How do you know what this little bundle of love is going to enjoy? Will they squeak at the sight of a fluffy bunny, freak out over a blue blanket or light up at the mere glimpse of the bathtub? At this early stage it is difficult to know where to start in pursuit of the perfect present. Take your inspiration from their star sign: even if you don't believe in the power of the planets, the characteristics associated with them can make for an amusing gift.

The **Aries** baby will endeavour to 'boldly go where no baby has ever gone before'. This is no sit-in-the-cot kid, quite the contrary, watch this little ram conquer the playroom and challenge the stairs. Bath time is a 'Journey to the Bottom of The Sea', a gripping tale of the lost city of Atlantis. Supply the necessary **bath toys** - slinky submarine, brightly coloured sea monsters and a water-shooting stun gun. Spice up car journeys by giving the budding dare devil racing-car driver his/her very own (**toy**) **steering wheel,** complete with knobs and switches and the all-important hooter accessory.

The self-conscious **Cancerian** can be shy, timid, retiring and, above all, sensitive. Like crabs, they retreat into their shells when threatened. So the typical Cancer kid would enjoy the snuggle comfort and security of a **playpen** or **nursery tent.** Another perfect present is a **wrap-up romper suit,** with a hood big enough to hide under. Above all, Cancerians are home-lovers, so for the crib-proud Cancerian give a glistening **initialled white blanket.** Alternatively, to help them practise those shy smiles, a special keepsake would be a tiny **hand mirror.**

The Lord-it-up **Leo** simply longs for the limelight and loves to be leader. This confident, positive pussy cat will just adore to be admired in a **funky floppy hat,** assuring his or her rightful position to be crowned as Lord or Lady of the prams. Luxury and comfort are at the top of the 'must have' list for this little cub, so a **red velvet cushion** embroidered with a golden emblem would make a perfect, princely present. A dressing gown with gold braid trimming will complete the royal regalia.

The typical **Taurus** tends to be conscientious, careful and determined. The consistent bull will be sure to accumulate collections like coins, stamps, matchboxes or beer mats in later life. So starting a collection of **classic children's books** would be just perfect for this horned hero. Sharing is this bull's red rag, games for one are far more appropriate and brightly coloured **wooden building bricks** will appeal to the productive and constructive Taurean character. But be warned, woe betide anyone who kicks over this kid's brick castle.

Gemini is the sign of duality or twins. The Gemini tot is investigative, adaptable and self-expressive. This is the baby who weighs up the pros and cons, carefully contemplating whether to scream the place down or laugh its head off. Present this baby with **two identical teddies,** so they can decide which one will accompany them to bed. Or fill their room with curiosity-quenching, scientifically-baffling toys such as **a mobile** that moves and plays a tune or an **interactive pop-up play book.**

If there were such a thing as a baby daily organizer, you can be sure this child would have one. The typical **Virgo** is bursting with common sense, intelligence and an insatiable appetite for precision planning. From an early age, games will be neatly stacked in original boxes and books catalogued according to colour. So why not buy this fastidious baby a **toy box?** Always in the pursuit of a problem to solve, a **shape posting game** will prove popular. They also love to plot and plan for the future, so **a savings account** would certainly meet with approval.

present ideas

♎ **Librans** are the masters of fair play; they methodically travel through life measuring up and justifying each and every situation. The little Libran will crave an even environment, their bedroom should neither be too cold nor too warm: **an ioniser or air humidifier** to balance the atmosphere would be a perfect offering. A **book of fairy tales or myths and legends** would encourage their inventive minds.

♏ Strong-willed **Scorpios** always get what they want from any given situation. They are fervently emotional, intensely passionate and possess a magnetic personality. They can be prone to the vice of vanity, so a loving offering for those impromptu public appearances is a flashy **travel changing mat and matching bag,** packed to the brim with the latest baby lotions and potions. The tiny Scorpio is inexhaustible in its search for knowledge, so any interactive, mind-stimulating toy such as a **cot-side activity centre,** complete with ringing bell, is a sure winner.

♐ The danger-seeking **Sagittarian** is in constant hot pursuit of the next exciting adventure. Driving at death-defying speed or gambling away their life savings is all in a day's play for this raring-to-go child. The baby Sagittarian will be bursting to explore, so the most practical gift for this boisterous babe is **a baby bouncer on wheels.** Variety is essential in this little one's life, so rather than one expensive item, buy **a collection of cheaper toys.**

♑ The careful, conscientious **Capricorn** is possessed with a will of iron. This toddler prefers sitting on the sidelines to joining in the whims of the world around them. To the introverted, misunderstood Capricorn, secret-keeping is second nature, so this little person is sure to appreciate a confidential **lockable keepsake box** and, later on, **a five-year diary with padlock and key.** Capricorns have an insatiable thirst for knowledge, so help their parents cope with the endless Why's and When's by providing the would-be scholar with an **illustrated encyclopaedia;** even if they can't read they'll enjoy the pictures.

♒ The typical **Aquarian** is idealistic, intuitive and generous. They are the first to fight for the rights of those less fortunate than themselves and a present directed not at them but at some needy creature is the answer here: **sponsor a refugee child or make them a member of an animal charity.** Traditional toys hold no water with the up-to-the-minute Aquarian, whose interest lies in new-fangled objects and complex scientifically devised contraptions. A **state-of-the-art baby buggy** with ergonomically designed reclining seat and precision steering is the only mode of transport for the Aquarian.

♓ **Pisces** are powerfully imaginative, kind-hearted and romantic but can veer onto the over-emotional side. The Piscean baby will need plenty of hugs and reassuring smiles so a tiny **T-shirt** with the words **"Tell Me You Love Me"** will provide them with a steady dose of the necessary encouragement. The pensive Piscean is perfectly happy to dream the day away, so for bedtime star-gazing, give them a pack of **luminous stars** for their ceiling.

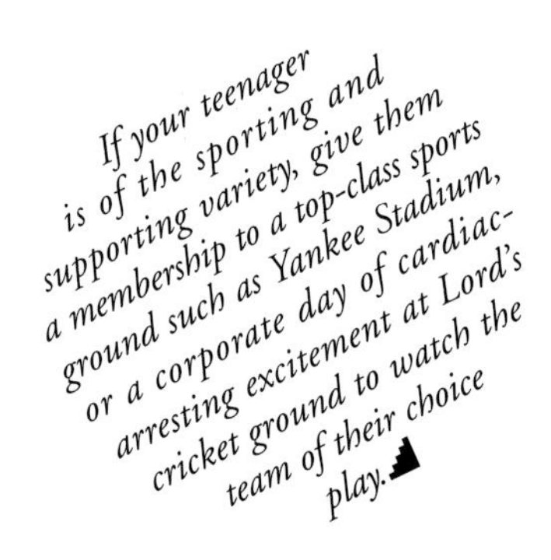

If your teenager is of the sporting and supporting variety, give them a membership to a top-class sports ground such as Yankee Stadium, or a corporate day of cardiac-arresting excitement at Lord's cricket ground to watch the team of their choice play.

teenager

ARRIVING *at their teens is the first real watershed in a child's life. The onset of adulthood is marked in almost every society by some ritual, be it religious or sexual, and this reminder of adult responsibilities (as well as freedom) around the corner can be enhanced by your gift.*

•H.R.H. *Prince Filipe of Spain's* most treasured present remains a telescope given to him by his grandmother for his twelflth birthday, the last present she gave him before she died. His grandmother knew of his early passion for the stars and his unfulfilled desire to study astrophysics. For him it represents what he could have done were he not destined to become king.

ONCE YOUR teenager is hit by the great hormonal surge known as adolescence, they'll have lots of changes thrust upon them. One thing you can encourage is the concept of money extending beyond next Saturday's installment. Teenage years may see your offspring taking up a part-time job, so **open a bank account** to encourage them to save their independent wealth.

THE TYPICAL teenager needs to be up-to-the-minute on all the pop reviews, fashion fads and gossip. Life depends on knowing the fast-moving facts, if they're going to maintain their street-cred. Supply them with the necessary manual, **a subscription to the hippest teen magazine around.**

THERE COMES a time when the deep bond between mother and daughter is shattered by their first confrontation. This may be brought on by her refusal to condone a nose ring or change of hair colour from dark chestnut to tomato-red.Compromise is the answer. Settle for **pierced ears**, a fine **pair of gold loops** and, if unavoidable, a **wig** in the desired hue.

SNAKES slithering down hotpants and live hamsters sacrificed on stage. Been there, seen it, done that. Rock concerts today pale into insignificance compared with the antics of yesteryear. So don't fret, dear parents, set them free with a couple of **rock concert tickets** for your trustworthy teenager.

WHY IS IT that teenagers prefer their own company to anyone else's? It seems they spend most of their time mooning in the dark solitude of their bedrooms, playing tracks from their favourite pop group. Their bedroom is their sanctuary, a retreat that is out-of-bounds to the rest of the world. Privacy is all they desire. Therefore the best present that you can give a teenager is **a padlock and key** for their bedroom door (can be used either inside or out).

TEENAGERS gravitate towards music like bimbos to make-up counters. If you don't want your living room filled with slumped adolescents listening to or watching their favourite music programmes, you'd better give in and buy them their own **hi-fi or TV.**

YOUR AVERAGE teenager gets spots, mood swings and a startling interest in the opposite sex. Suddenly girls are to be blushed at and boys are a source of fascination. Hmm, in fact, they turn out to be kind of interesting, er, better ask for their phone number. A **little black address book**, in classic or Filofax form, will provide them with the perfect dating aid.

THIS IS A time when they suddenly become aware of the effect their surroundings can have on their friends. If they want to be seen to be cool, down come all the cartoon posters and the pretty wallpaper and prints of childhood in favour of the sofabed and low lighting. If your gloomy adolescent hankers after a black hole or the moody blues, indulge them with **a trip to the DIY centre** and equip them with the required **paint and brushes.**

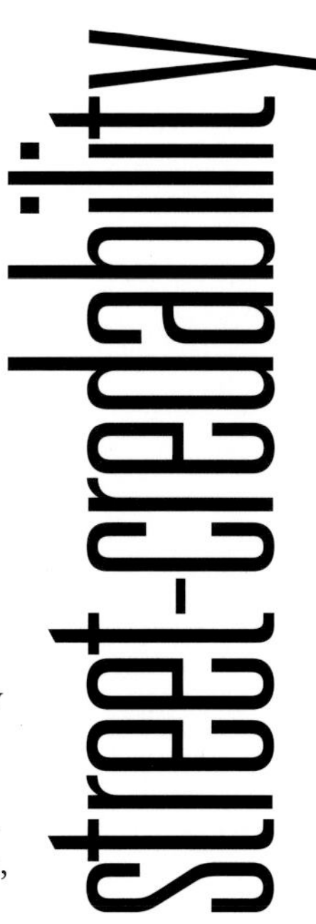

graduation

CONSIDERING *what the average student has to go through to gain a decent set of results, it's amazing that they survive at all - the pressure is monumental; the hours they study are totally uncivilized and the food consumed, enough to turn any health fanatic in their grave. Good results deserve more than a piece of paper.*

A RECURRING nightmare for all about-to-be-employed people is the fear of oversleeping on that all-important first morning. Replace the Mickey Mouse child's clock with a flash new **digital alarm clock with radio**, so they'll be both on time and ahead of the news.

IF YOUR graduate has managed to step straight onto the first rung of the career ladder, then congratulations are certainly in order. But they might still need some help to metamorphose from student-union wit into serious, power-dressing, career-minded executive. Smarten up their image with a **briefcase**, a **top-of-the-range pen** or some **stylish desk accessories.**

YOUR DEAREST young adult has made it through their final exams. Complete with mortarboard, billowing black cape and certificate proudly in hand, they are ready to steer into life's fast lane, so it would be helpful if they knew how to drive. **A set of L-plates** and **a course of driving lessons** is the best way to set them on the road to success.

THOSE SPORTING trophies and records broken are liable to become a thing of the past once they discover the delights of late night fun and have to combine it with long days at the office. To prevent your young god or goddess becoming a fully fledged couch potato, give them **a membership to the coolest gym or the trendiest sports club** in their area.

STUDENT = penniless = overdraft: the inevitable downward curve of graduate finances. Now they've achieved the desired results, give them a break and a clean financial slate by **paying off their debts** upon their graduation.

POST GRADUATION, the next step to becoming a complete and socially acceptable adult is to pin down that first job. In this increasingly difficult endeavour it is essential to have a curriculum vitae of a quality immensely superior to those of the competition. For the high-flyer of the future, why not offer to pay for the **professional compilation of their c.v.?**

leaving home

YEARN FOR *it we do, but when push comes to shove the finality of leaving home is actually rather scary. Who will cook, wash up, do the laundry, protect and care for us through thick and thin? Before you finally kick the fledgelings out of the nest, present them with a few necessary aids to survival.*

TAKEAWAYS are great when you're a child and fed up with your mother's 'real food', but the novelty palls and your expenses rise if you rely on them as staple meals in your first home away from home. To prevent your young one from starving to death whilst finding his or her feet out there, provide them with **a month's supply of food.**

THOSE packets and tins may keep them going for a while, but you want them to make a habit of eating properly. Give them some encouragement with a **cookery course** or **a step-by-step beginner's cookbook** to start them on the gourmet trail.

INDEPENDENT they may be, grown up they certainly think they are, but it's guaranteed they'll see no reason why they shouldn't bring you home their dirty washing on a regular basis. If you are inured to this fate, at least give them a **large linen bag** so you don't have to cope with those grubby plastic carriers (preferably with a name and address tag for when they leave it on the bus or train).

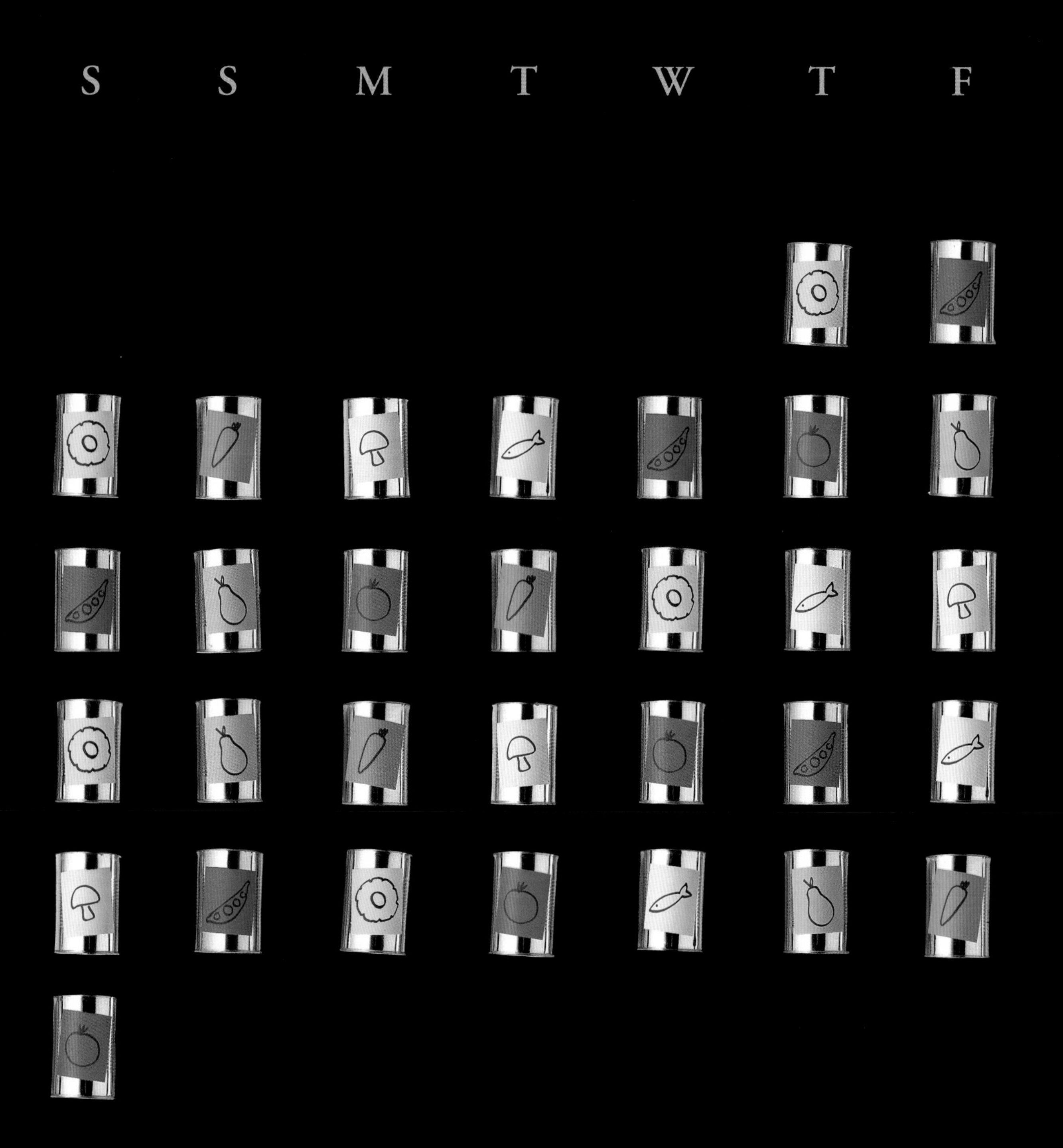

To prevent your recently departed young one from starving to death, provide them with ***a month's supply of food.*** ❤ ♛

divorce or separation

Breaking up *is so hard to do. The one who departs feels inevitably guilty, whilst for the one who is left, separation leaves a gaping void in their life. If you have a recently divorced friend, don't leave them moping on the sofa, one hand in the box of tissues and the other clutched to the phone pouring out their woes to their friends. Try to convince them that this can be a new beginning.*

One practical thing you can do for them is to open their eyes to possibilities beyond the bounds of disharmonic domesticity and **send them prospectuses on courses, group activities and new hobbies.**

She or he refuses to be consoled, convinced that spaghetti *à deux* in front of the television was always better than being escorted out by a new date. If you, being their dearest friend, are going to have to sit through hours of misery, it's infinitely better to do it in agreeable surroundings. Agree to pick them up at 8.00 p.m. and tell them to dress up, then take them off for **dinner at the smartest restaurant in town**. Comfort food and a glass of wine, with the added bonus of heads turning as they enter and leave the establishment, might even get your friend thinking that the single life ain't so bad…❤

Instead of looking back through rose-tinted glasses on those early days of bliss as a twosome, remind them of the carefree joys of the single life. Buy **a diary**, gather mutual friends and fill your lonely friend's week with a **whirlwind of social engagements**.❤

Even if the divorce is amicable, there is always the problem of who is going to be awarded the family photo albums. These are one of the items that belong fairly and squarely to both sides, so who takes them? A great solution is to make up a **set of duplicate albums** and give them to your ex as a placatory gesture. Some possessions cannot be divided between a separating couple. What about the **library of books**, the **CDs and cassettes**? How on earth do you dissect the collection? The simple truth is that you can't. There is only one solution to this dilemma and that is to buy them a **duplicate collection.**❤

breaking-up

He might be great at smoothing lawns, but whoever he is, the betting is he has no idea how to produce a crinklefree shirt. Give him a helping hand and buy him **an iron** to restart him in his single life. For the lady in the dissolution, vision will be blinkered when it comes to those handy **power tools**. A foolish woman may take this gift as an insult to her femininity, but come the day her shelves collapse, she will thank her lucky stars that she has such a practical friend.

It would be very easy to sling a sexist slant on this idea by implying that it was aimed only at a divorced man. Naturally we would not even consider doing anything so politically incorrect!

Cooking lessons, books or a set of favourite (easy) recipes would be most useful to both parties undergoing a separation, as years of togetherness have made it almost impossible for either of them to cook as a single person!

The divorce papers have come through. This may be cause for commiseration or celebration. Either way it marks the end of an era, the beginning of a new age and should be celebrated as such in a positive way. Take round **a bottle of champagne** and allow your friend either to drown their sorrows or kick up their heels.

Provide your departing partner with a duplicate set of photo albums.

Golden Oldie is an affectionate term, symbolizing respect, love and affection for someone who is, let us say, more mature in outlook. So, when does someone actually start qualifying for a Golden Oldie tag? In reality it is less a reaching of age than a reflection of status in life - retired, grandparent, or beloved older friend. But take care when choosing Golden Oldie gifts.

It is acceptable to give presents that are on the sentimental side, as long as they don't offend the intellect.

AGILE FRAGILE FRAGILE FRAGILE

Another important thing to remember is that growing older doesn't automatically involve a total loss of sense of humour; grey hair on the outside doesn't necessarily mean loss of grey matter on the inside. The only difference in our outlook as we grow older is that we tend to become more affiliative and like to feel part of a group.

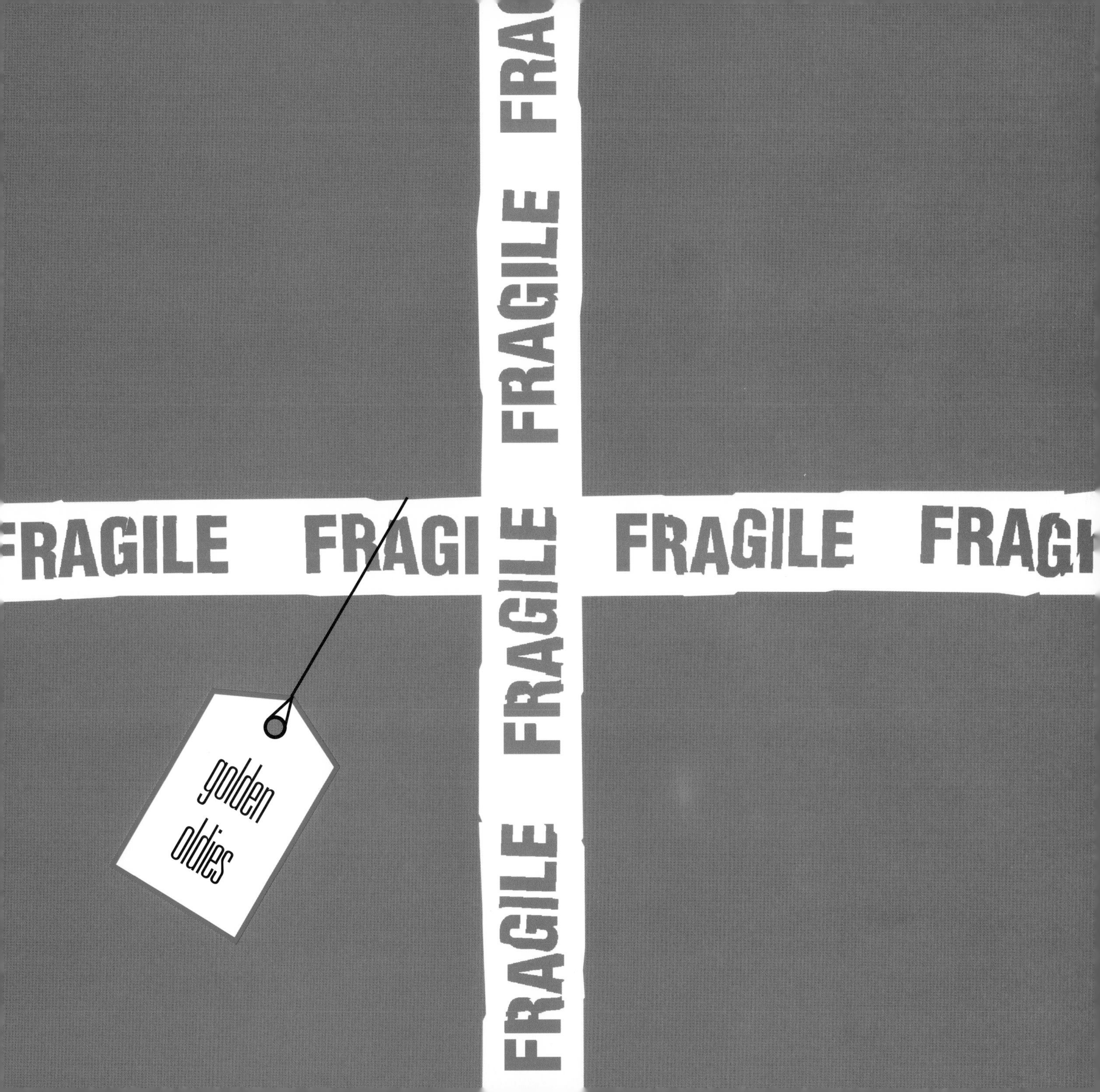
FRAGILE FRAGILE FRAGILE
golden oldies

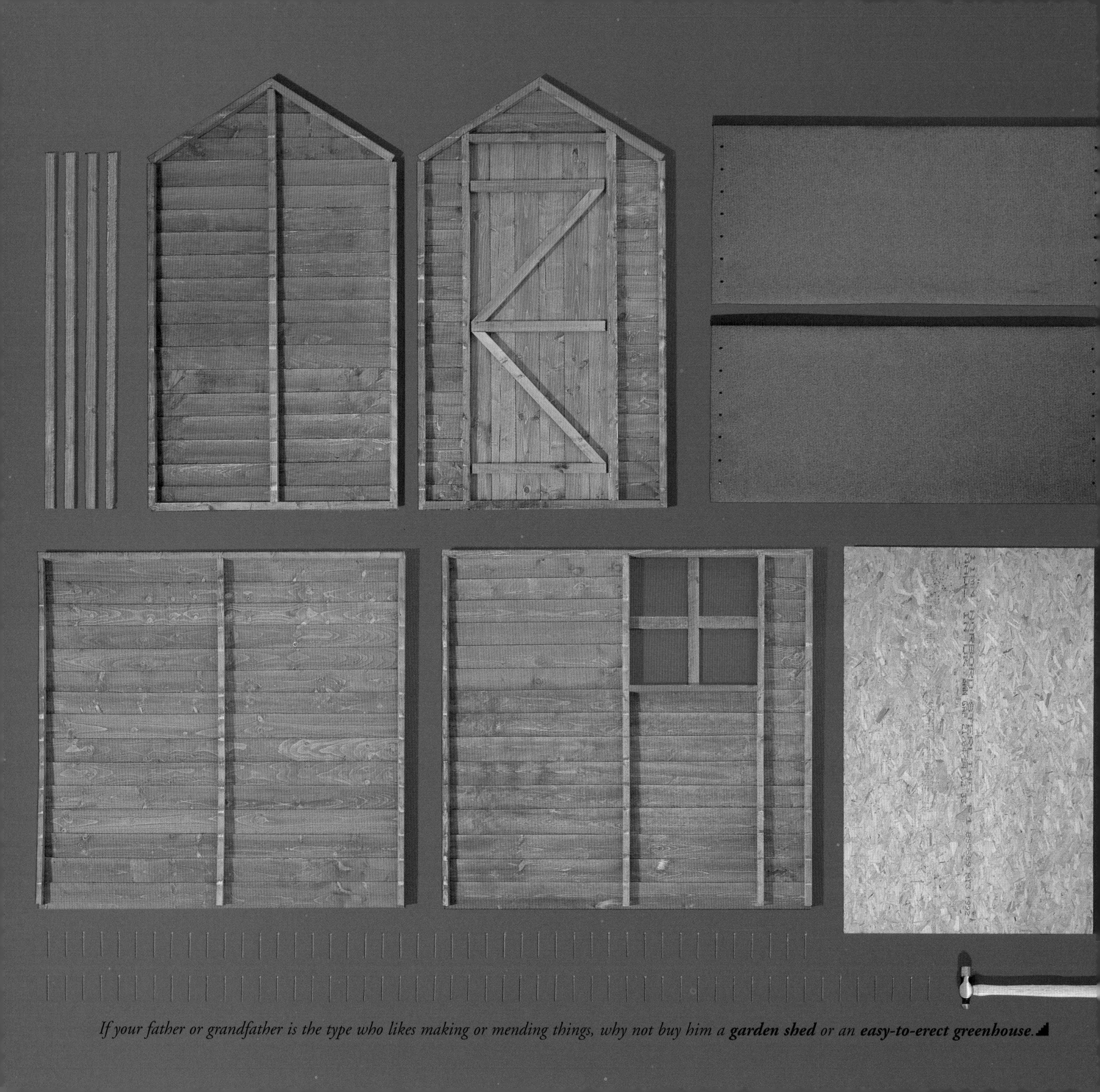
If your father or grandfather is the type who likes making or mending things, why not buy him a ***garden shed*** *or an* ***easy-to-erect greenhouse.***

retirement

Retirement *brings with it a wild array of emotions. Some people relish having time to themselves, while others dread the possibility of being bored. Retirement should in any case be looked on as an exciting new beginning, and this should be reflected in the attitudes of all friends, family and loved ones. At last, after putting in a lifetime's service, they can settle down to a well-deserved rest followed by time spent doing the things they've always wanted to do but never had the time. Whether it's by encouraging a new venture, supplying an adventure or helping to fulfil a dream, well-chosen gifts can be the key to a successful retirement.*

After all those years at the centre of events, the quiet life will be quite a culture shock and he or she may suddenly feel as if they're losing touch with what's going on in the world. Enable them to keep *au fait* with the action by buying them **a magazine subscription** in their chosen field or in world affairs.

If your mother, aunt or friend has always wanted to create a wonderful garden but has always been too busy, now is the time to indulge her passion. **Subscribe,** on her behalf, to **a gardening book club** and to the best **horticultural society,** who will also give her details of gardens to visit for inspiration.

When an oldie steps off the work treadmill, it can feel as if the ground has been removed from under their feet. It is vital during this period of disorientation that they keep active rather than becoming a depressed and wrinkly couch potato. Not only is keeping fit a great tonic for the blues, but it is a great way for anyone, not just the older generation, to combat ill-health and low energy levels. Supply them with a tonic in the form of **a temporary membership to the local health club or country club** where they can choose their preferred activities according to their energy level (or just sit in the bar and make new friends).

If your mother, grand-mother or friend has just retired, then a brilliant way to symbolize the end of her old working life and the positive beginning of her new leisurely one is to **treat her to a relaxing day at the beauty salon and hairdresser**. This is also always a good gift for any special occasion, such as Mother's Day or her birthday.

hobbies

We all make plans for skills we want to learn or subjects we want to know more about throughout our lives, but the majority are put on the back burner until we have 'more time'. When it comes to this time, however, we've often forgotten where to start. Here is an area where friends can be encouraging. Do a little gentle digging to find out what their interests might be, then **research all the courses** and have the brochures sent direct for them to take their pick.

It may not even be necessary to interrogate them to find out their interest. Hidden away in a cupboard or the loft might be a carefully packed box with their old collection, be it stamps, coins or silver, that they've had no time to add to for years. Get those acquisitive juices going again with **a new key item for their collection,** or **the latest reference book** on the subject, and watch the twinkle come back into their eyes.

do-it-yourself

Yes, of course your parents still adore one another, they don't really want to get away from each other, but having him around all day is driving your mother up the wall. If your father or grandfather is the type who likes making or mending things, or is passionate about plants, give him a bit of space to indulge his hobby. Buy him a **garden shed** or an **easy-to-erect greenhouse.**

out to grass

As fascinating as your **grandfather's stories** may be, they are definitely suffering a little from verbal overexposure. But in years to come, will you be able to remember all the details in order to pass them on to your children? Keep a record of your family history and give grandfather a new lease of life by persuading him to record the adventures of his life for posterity. Give him **a blank journal, a tape recorder with plenty of cassettes** (or, for the up-to-the-minute man, **a laptop computer**). Who knows, one day they might be considered important enough to publish.

Extraordinary as it may seem, some people actually enjoy hitting a small pimply white ball across the countryside and retrieving it, ad nauseum. Golf may not be your passion, but it is a great game for retirement, providing exercise, companionship and lots of fresh air. For those who are out on the green in fair weather or foul, one necessity will be a constant supply of balls. To celebrate their successful arrival at the age of retirement, give the budding Ballesteros a gift of **65 golf balls** (or the appropriate number if they were lucky enough to retire early).

The older generation has not yet cottoned on to the absolute necessity of keeping in touch by phone. Having been out all day at work they are used to leaving the telephone ringing in an empty house. Now, however, with all those potential social engagements, they will realize the usefulness of an **answerphone**. On the next occasion you can give them **a portable phone**, to prevent them scurrying from one end of the house to the other to catch that vital call.

Another surefire winner for old age is **bridge**, a game which keeps one amused for hours and, whilst not exactly exercising the body, certainly stimulates the brain. If your oldies would like to learn, **enrol them in the local bridge club**. If they are already players, keep them keen with **a card table.**

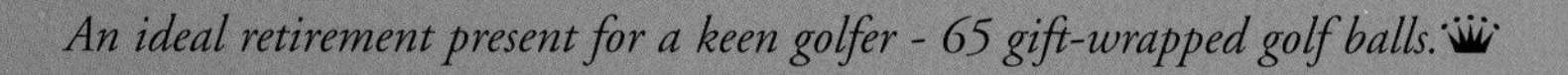

An ideal retirement present for a keen golfer - 65 gift-wrapped golf balls.

birthday surprise

ONCE ONE has retired from work, it's time to get down to some serious correspondence. But rather than endless longhand letters to those relatives overseas, what better than a **dictaphone or cassette recorder**, on which they can record family news in a more immediate way to send to friends and family members abroad.❤

TO START off their retirement in the required spirit of leisure, suggest and organise **a weekend break** for them. It may be Paris, it may be Rome, or, if they are on their own, it might be that they would prefer a **weekend at your own home** to enjoy a taste of family life, real home cooking and some well-earned pampering.❤

NOW THEIR home has become more than a place to sleep and relax after the stresses and strains of a long day at the office, the betting is they will begin to look at it with new eyes. They will have time to make all those little changes they've wanted over the years and **home improvement** will soon become an enjoyable pastime. Gadgets of every sort appeal to this generation, so scour those catalogues full of innovative ideas to provide them with the latest dust-collectors, window-fasteners, chair-hoovers and other peculiar new-fangled cleaning aids.♛

IN SIMILAR vein, a whole new world could be opened up with the gift of a **DIY work bench**. This also opens up endless possibilities for future gifts with the latest, **state-of-the-art tools and equipment**.▟♛

YOUR FATHER retired a month ago and the house is already suffering from an overdose of DIY. It's time to divert his attention to outside pursuits, no doubt the garden could do with a bit of an overhaul. Give him the ultimate in garden toys, an **electric strimmer**: a tidy-up power tool that requires skill, careful handling and, of course, the all-important **protective goggles**.▟♛

IF YOUR happy-go-lucky retired friends have decided to up sticks and move to pastures new, don't let them depart without a well-stocked **photograph album** complete with loving messages from all their family and friends.❤

WE ALL look forward to a troublefree retirement, but only on condition that our health won't let us down. If they haven't thought of it and you can afford it, **medical welfare and health insurance** would be a generous gesture which will enable them to enjoy their newfound freedom without worries.♛

Flowers for retirement
Campanula, White - Gratitude
Indian Azalea - True to the end
Periwinkle, White - Pleasures of memory
Stock - Lasting beauty
Sage - Esteem

NEVER TAKE *the words "I don't celebrate birthdays at my age" seriously. Birthdays are indelibly marked in everyone's heart and, whatever they may say, they will want the occasion recognized, even with a gesture. Woe betide you if you ever forget to send at the very least a card or the customary bunch of blooms. Despite their protestations that they've got everything they need, this may well not be the case. Failing eyesight and increased lack of mobility, in themselves, provide the younger members of the family with opportunities to give gifts which will genuinely improve their quality of life.*

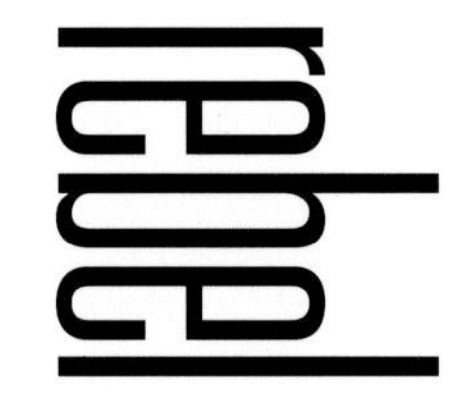

DON'T BE misled by the tradition that dictates that all elderly people are fragile, faint at the sound of a swear word and don't like being driven over the speed limit. It is not strictly true. There is an element to old age that brings out the rebel in many grandpersons. So don't shy away from doing the unexpected. **A bit of lighthearted gambling or a day out at the races** will give them a welcome change of scene and get those hearts racing as they cheer their favourite home.▟♛

FOR THOSE who love reading in bed but are now having trouble with adequate lighting, provide them with **a clip-on anglepoise lamp for the bedhead**.♛

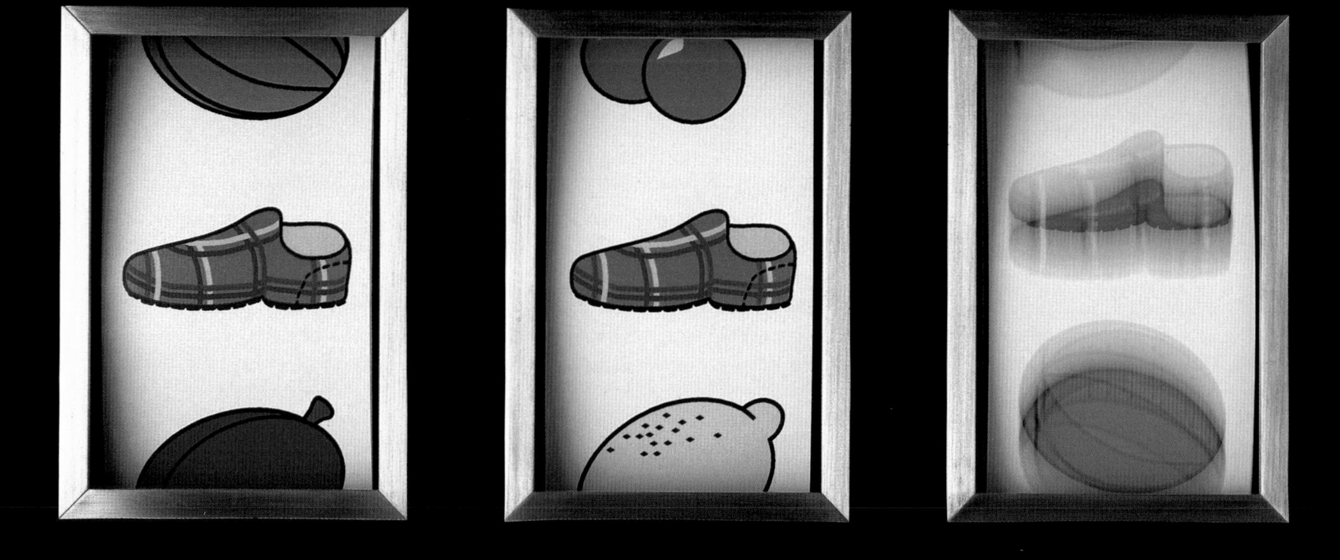

Bring the rebel out in your grandparents; a bit of lighthearted gambling will give them a change of scene and get their hearts racing.

birthday treat

A MICROWAVE can revolutionize eating habits as well as saving on the boring old washing-up. Hot chocolate in a cup, scrambled egg in a bowl and not a saucepan in sight! Revolutionise your oldies' kitchen with this up-to-the-minute appliance. (Hint: supply them with a good **microwave cookbook** to get them going.)♛

HOME *is* where the heart is, and your parents would probably love to know more about the place where they live. **Research their house's history** or that of the local area and present them with a scrapbook or collage of old photographs to put their ~~dwelling~~ in context.❤

DURING ONE of those long hot summers when every detail of the land can be seen, commission an **aerial photo of their home.** Better still, give them the flight (or fright) of their lives with **a hot air balloon ride**, for a bird's-eye view of the places they love.❤

THE CAR may be the first sacrifice an older person has to make. The pleasure of simply exploring the delights of the nearest town or city, checking out the latest art exhibitions, catching a musical, or taking in a film, may now have to be crossed off the social agenda, let alone the difficulty of doing the weekly shop. Give them a boost and arrange for a once a week/ fortnight /month **taxi fare to anywhere they want to go** (within reason of course). No more trudging home on the bus or relying on you to ferry them home after dark.♛

NOTHING is more irritating for those who love reading than the discovery that the print in their favourite books is mysteriously growing smaller and that their cherished hobby is becoming an impossibility. Enable them to save their eyes for necessities and **join a library of talking books** on their behalf. It will also save them the trips to and fro their library or bookshop with a heavy load.♛

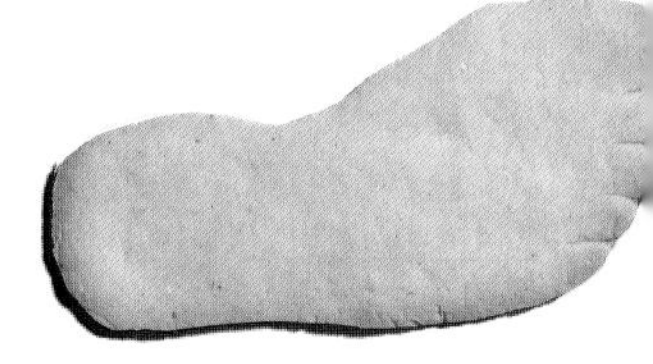

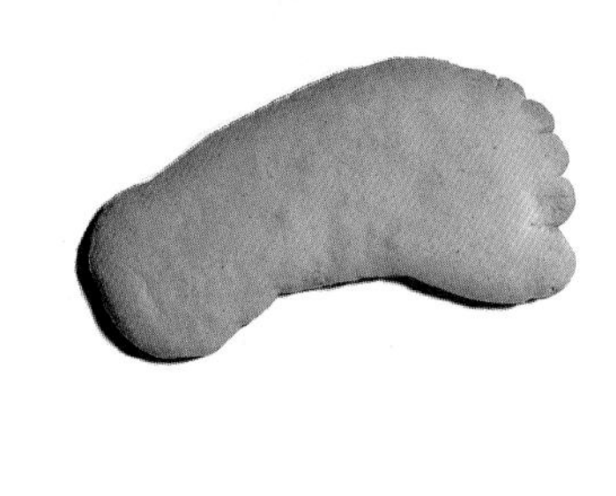

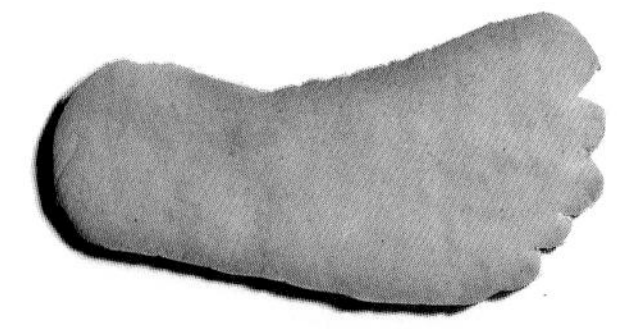

Biscuits baked in the shape of grandchildren's hands and feet will be a sure hit with Granny and Grandpa.❤

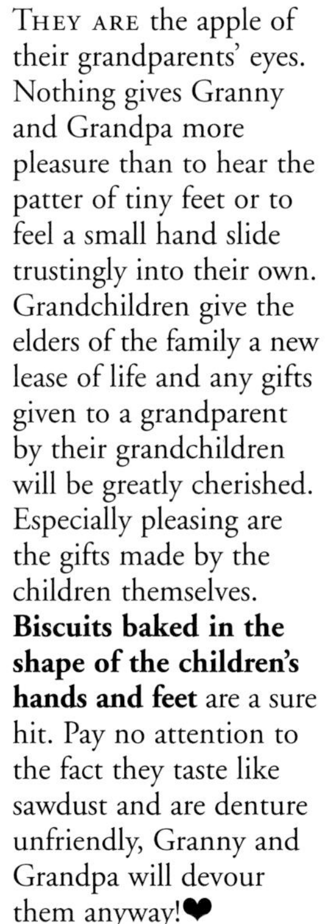

They are the apple of their grandparents' eyes. Nothing gives Granny and Grandpa more pleasure than to hear the patter of tiny feet or to feel a small hand slide trustingly into their own. Grandchildren give the elders of the family a new lease of life and any gifts given to a grandparent by their grandchildren will be greatly cherished. Especially pleasing are the gifts made by the children themselves. **Biscuits baked in the shape of the children's hands and feet** are a sure hit. Pay no attention to the fact they taste like sawdust and are denture unfriendly, Granny and Grandpa will devour them anyway!❤

There is nothing like an alcoholic tipple to get the oldies revved up and chirping. It is likely that every time you visit them, the inevitable bottle of sherry is brought out. Can you imagine their pride in offering a glass of wine grown from their own vine? Seems a little far-fetched? In fact it is possible to **rent a row of vines** from which the grapes can be processed into a bottle with a customised label. (Hint: Ask your local wine merchant)

Remember those agonisingly embarrassing **cine films** of you making a sandcastle (naked) on the beach, and how the **photos** of your first dribbling smiles were proudly shown to every prospective husband who walked through the front door? That very same source of adolescent embarrassment may just be the answer to your gift dilemma. Set ego aside, secretly acquire the aforementioned films and snaps and despatch them to your friendly photo lab to be magically **transferred onto video** format.❤

Children have a wonderful view of the world so who better to **commission to do a portrait of your parents** than the budding family Picasso, **your child**. Signed by the artist and framed, it will be a birthday present that will take pride of place on their wall.❤

Visiting grandparents is something we should all do as often as possible. But how many times have you realised that months have slipped past, without even a letter from you to inform them of the (exciting to them, boring to you) new developments in your life? Birthdays are an obligatory visiting occasion, so supply them with a little coffee-table reading matter. Find **a large display portfolio** and fill the pages with photos, letters and other paraphernalia, summing up **your life to the present day**. This could become a regular birthday feature, and never again hearing the words "We never know what you get up to" will be well worth the effort you make.❤

For the gift of a lifetime, get all the family to club together and send the parents or grandparents on a cruise.

milestones

WHEN YOUR *age has well and truly spanned every shoe size, dress size and chest size, birthdays tend to lose their excitement until the landmarks of 70, 80, 90 then, maybe, 100 heave into view. These are serious birthdays indeed and must be celebrated with all the appropriate solemnity and gifts to match the occasion.*❤

THROWING **a party** is a must if you're sure the person for whom it is being arranged enjoys being the centre of attention. For a celebration of this importance, you might have to go to a bit more trouble than usual. Find all their **old friends from the past** and, most importantly, keep it **a real surprise**. The result will be worth it: tears of joy intermingled with tears of laughter, as the happily reunited friends chatter and reminisce the day away.❤

SURPRISE the birthday girl on the morning of this important day with a delivery of **70, 80, 90 or 100 of her favourite flowers.** The sheer mass of blooms, their colour and scent will really take her breath away.❤

AS YOU GROW older, you also grow tired of jetting from one place to another with an entourage of heavy suitcases, but you never grow sick of seeing the world. For the present of a lifetime, get all the family to club together and **send the parents or grandparents on a cruise**: by ship is still one of the most romantic ways to travel, getting spoiled all day long is everyone's idea of heaven.❤

TRACING A **family tree**, it has to be said, is not an overnight task. Months can be spent tracking, writing to and phoning just one name, only to find a red herring on the end of the line. So if you'd like to increase the self-importance of your aged relative and place him firmly at the head of his branch of the family, consider engaging the services of an expert. For a fee, a genealogist will piece together your family ancestry. Armed with this vital information, track down those living, long-lost relatives and ask them to send photos of themselves, then frame all the findings and present the entire package as an **instant family gallery**. Compound the surprise by inviting those who can to the birthday celebration at which it's unveiled.❤

throw a party

Blockbuster anniversaries

WHEN YOUR wedding anniversary has passed the coral mark, it becomes the property of the entire family and, of course, can be held up as a shining example to the rest of the world that marriage does actually work. Much ado should be made of sub-sequent wedding anniversaries. The older the marriage gets, the greater the achievement and the larger the rewards in terms of gifts.

30th - Pearl
35th - Coral
40th - Ruby
45th - Sapphire
50th - Gold
55th - Emerald
60th - Diamond
75th - Double Diamond

You don't have to be rich to find a present that will be appreciated, just use a bit of imagination. Here are some ideas which can be adapted for any of the above:

Golden Anniversary

A pair of inscribed **gold-rimmed glasses or decanter**.
A photograph album edged with **gold leaf** containing a pictorial resumé of their marriage (try to find old love letters, engagement photographs, the marriage service, photos of the children, their pets, their homes etc).
A **gilded table lamp or candelabra.**
Luxury chocolates wrapped in golden foil and tied with a golden bow (good from the grandchildren).
A bouquet of **50 golden flowers**.
Gilded photo frames for all the family photos.
Golden coins from the year of their wedding.
Get everyone in the family to give something made of **gold**, have it **melted down** and turned into **two rings, a bowl** or a **spoon**.

Diamond Anniversary

Diamond **cuff-links** for him, diamond **studs** for her.
A solid **crystal set of glasses or fruit bowl.**
Crystalline **flowers of sparkling white** - roses, lilies, jasmine, stephanotis.
Borrow their watches and have a **diamond set into each winder**.
A **crystal chandelier.**
Shares in a diamond mine.

The milk of human kindness has a tendency to dry up when we fall victim to a scornful attack. The ultimate gesture, of course, is to forgive and forget, which is precisely what we should do… just as soon as we get even!

Maybe it seems a bit of a contradiction in terms to give a present to someone you don't even like. However, there are different degrees of 'don't like': there are those whom we genuinely can't stand but to whom we cannot avoid ritual gift giving (meddling relatives, boyfriend's ex-girlfriends, difficult in-laws).

Then there are friends (or erstwhile friends) who have done us wrong and should know better. Finally, there are those who slightly irritate us by their presence and in our opinion need taking down a peg or two. For these last two categories the art of subtle gift giving can be a powerful tool in righting a wrong.

people you
don't really like

ex-lovers

The grown-up *thing to do is to walk away from a failed relationship with your head held high, your dignity intact and narry so much as a backward glance. However, a little nip of gentle revenge goes an awfully long way to help mend a shattered heart. So, keep your cool, think before you act, then calmly despatch a gift with ego-shattering aim.*

Your ex-lover may be streetwise and charming, but not included in his list of skills is how to walk out of a relationship with consideration. Why not give him a few tips on how to do it properly with a cassette recording of Paul Simon's classic hit ***Fifty Ways To Leave Your Lover.*** Maybe next time he'll at least "Drop off the key, Lee".

Valentine's Day is approaching. Not that you care, but the shops keep on reminding you. Everyone else seems to be in a relationship apart from you, otherwise why would all those millions of red roses suddenly have appeared in the florists? You certainly don't have any use for them - or do you? Your girlfriend's departure into the arms of your best friend is a horror story of suicidal proportions. The following suggestion will not succeed in bringing her back, but it will satisfy some of those vindictive thoughts you have been harbouring. As soon as those flowers hit the stands, buy a generous bunch, then watch them wilt until V-day arrives. The **dead roses** delivered with your signature will say it all.

You've been dumped. It's okay, you can handle it. You don't mind being just good friends. This time you are going to be really mature about it. You will refrain from bombarding him with silent phone calls, you will invite him and his new girlfriend for a cosy supper and, hey, you will even go to the trouble of finding him a special gift for his first birthday without you. As your ex, he will not be surprised to receive an intimate present like **a pair of boxer** or jockey shorts. However, these will have that unexpected little extra that only he will discover and whether he thanks you remains to be seen. Before you send them, nip down to the joke shop and purchase some **itching powder**, then liberally sprinkle over your gift.

This section *is dedicated to the ego eradication of those annoying people that dare to challenge the equilibrium of your relationship. Some of them mean no real harm and the best response is to ignore their advancing tactics. However, there are those who appear to enjoy testing the limits of your self-restraint and they must be dealt with.*

Sometimes your boyfriend feels an inexplicable loyalty to an ex-girlfriend or a doe-eyed girl who, as he puts it, is 'just a friend'. Is it flattery or stupidity that blinds him to the truth? Girls like this have a tendency to turn up at the most irritating times or continue to loiter around after the last person has left following a party at his home. It all seems very harmless on the surface, but you know better: these innocent little incidents are all part of a master plan to get her grubby little mitts on your man. So, when he drags you to her birthday party, you have the perfect opportunity to give her a little token that shows she can't fool you. A **red leather manicure set** with a note saying: "Sharpen your claws!" will make it perfectly clear you mean business.

Enough is enough! That girl is not only in hot pursuit of your beloved, but she's stooping to the pathetic trapping tactic of copying your personal style. Does she think that dressing like you will magically divert his adoring eyes from you to her? Take this chance to turn out your cupboards and give her a **bag full of all your old clothes.** After all, if she wants to style herself on you, the least you can do is give her the benefit of your impeccable fashion advice.

*A bunch of **dead flowers** delivered to your ex-lover on Valentine's Day will say it all.*

If you are the victim of an office nosy parker, let them know that you are onto them with a stunningly simple and symbolic token. When they unwrap their mystery gift to discover a spyglass they will be momentarily perplexed, but it won't take long before they're blushing to the roots of their hair. Rumbled!

workplaCE

THIS *is where we spend a large percentage of our precious time. While managing to sail along quite happily with the majority of our colleagues, there are those who seem determined to rock the boat. Lazy, bossy, smug, unreasonable and big-headed are the predominant characteristics that would appear on these people's c.v.'s. How can you subtly point out their imperfections, without destroying the harmonious atmosphere of the office? Gifts,of course! The materialisation of a surprise package on the offending desk can be a powerful course of action that will speak far louder than the harshest words.*

BREATHING OVER you while you're trying to use the photocopier and nestling up close to peruse a document are sure signs that you're the target of **the office lecher**. Whilst this behaviour does not exactly qualify as sexual harassment, it is definitely an unwelcome invasion of personal space. Give him short shrift with a well-aimed little gift and **a lesson in personal hygiene**. An obvious and brightly wrapped parcel in his in-tray will reveal some stain-removing toothpaste, mouthwash and a packet of 'odour-eating' inner soles.

mother-in-law

THE LIKELIHOOD *of acquiring a mother-in-law or stepmother that you dislike in this day and age is remote, but if you're the unlucky one this traditional hatred and jealousy is more often than not mutual and you can resign yourself to the fact that the relationship will be confrontational. As a matter of fact, you can get a lot of enjoyment out of being on the warpath with them. What better occasion to get your own back, or express some of your politely repressed feelings, than on your stepmother's birthday or with the obligatory thank-you present to your mother-in-law.*

WITH FAMILY, you can't avoid giving a present and you don't want to be labelled a cheapskate either. The one good thing in this instance about presents chosen for your family is that they feel bound to display them. So why not choose **something large and obtrusive** that unfortunately happens **to clash with her home**: a hideous ornament, a beastly vase or a tasteless picture, for instance. The important thing here is that it is big and doesn't fit in the back of a handy drawer.

A COMMON trait of mothers-in-law is **severe bossiness**. As far as they are concerned anyone younger than them is still in the throes of adolescence and therefore needs continual guidance, projected in the form of military-style orders. To help make the puppet dictator's life easier, present her with **a whistle**, of the silver, antique or plain old plastic variety.

DECIDING ON a gift for your **wicked stepmother** is time you would rather spend on a more pleasant pursuit. However, it's a task that has to be thought out and performed. So, this year, give her something that your father will love and that she simply can't snub: a large **framed photograph of yourself** - with the biggest superficial smile you can muster for the camera.

A CHARMING **photographic montage** depicting a year in the life of the entire family is a gift that will be treasured for ever by the in-laws. Pictures of young Jimmy on Grandpa's knee, naughty Helen with ice cream smeared all over her angelic face, mother and father frolicking with their offspring in a field of flowers and Bozo the dog digging up a bone, are all combined in a carefully framed collage. This is a gift that will surely hang in a prominent position on the kitchen wall. Too nice for the monster-in-law? Don't fret, it will soon become crystal clear that **a photograph of her is nowhere to be seen.**

wicked stepmother

IS YOUR mother-in-law a real stirrer in the family? Always meddling in other people's affairs? Trying to turn your husband/wife against you? Then this could be the ideal gift for her, especially if she likes cooking: a **giant wooden spoon**. Although both decorative and useful, the real meaning of the gift will hopefully not be lost on her.

poisonous

CHRISTMAS at the in-laws is over. Thank God. You have survived. Your marriage is still intact. Your children still have four limbs and it wasn't necessary to have your stomach pumped. As an insult to her cooking, show your appreciation by sending your charming mother-in-law a thank-you present in the form of **a step-by-step cookery course.**

Flowers for people you don't like

Carnation - Disdain
Hellebore - Scandal
Hydrangea - Heartlessness
Lobelia - Malevolence
Narcissus - Egotism
Nettle - Slander
Nightshade - Dark thoughts
Pennyroyal - Flee away
Pine - Pity
Scabious - Unfortunate attachment
Yellow rose - Infidelity
Venus Fly Trap - Deceit
Weeping Willow - Forsaken
Winter cherry - Deception

disloyal friend

Incredible *though it may seem, friends can descend to the depths of disloyalty on some occasions. When this happens you feel shocked by their betrayal. The strange thing is that you will probably forgive them, but only after you have demonstrated your wrath either face to face or in the form of a gift that spells out your displeasure.*

When a friend has let you down, you should teach them a lesson, to demonstrate the value of trust and loyalty. Here is one effective way. **Buy fourteen shell-on fresh prawns** and hide them to fester in your friend's flat. Then tell them you hid fifteen and watch them crawl around in desperation. How long you want this charade to go on for depends entirely on the quality of your mercy.

You have heard through the grapevine that a certain person has been spinning hurtful yarns at your expense. The content of their tittle-tattle is totally distorted, so before it becomes down-right defamatory, give them a warning. A charm or keyring in the shape of a pair of **ice skates,** accompanied by a note saying "You are walking on thin ice", should do the trick.

The gossip has got back to you and the source is, staggeringly, one of your best friends. Don't suffer in silence. Send them a **set of knives** to show that you are fully aware that they have been stabbing you in the back.

frustrating friend

There are *moments when you could simply throw in the towel of friendship over the imbecilic behaviour of a close friend. Although their frustrating behaviour doesn't deserve a real snub, you need to make your feelings known. To get your friendship back on course, challenge their intelligence and sense of humour with a little gift-giving test.*

In every group of friends there is always one who has it all. His meteoric rise in life seems to be unstoppable and he has done it again. He has just landed the most incredible job that has placed him in a different league. Congratulations are, of course, in order, that's if you could squeeze a word into his boasting monologue. It's time to test his (also boasted about) legendary sense of humour. Get all his mates to club together for the purchase of a **vast bouquet of pink blooms**, to be sent to his new office on the day that he starts this important job. The card attached must be big and visible and read: **"Darling (Johnnie), impress them all, you clever little bunny - Big Kiss xxx Mummy".**

A friend of yours is going through one of those irritating phases when she truly believes **the whole world revolves around her**. Yes, she is gorgeous, but not to the degree that she inflatedly assumes. As a friend, give her a helping hand down from these lofty heights, before she falls flat on her flawless face. **An exercise video** promising to remove 'all those unsightly bulges' is the perfect way to remind her that, alas, she too is mere flesh and blood.

A friend of yours has fallen under the spell of a new girlfriend who has decided, on his behalf, that he must change all his friends, how he dresses, where he goes and even what he eats! Suddenly you and your friends never see him anymore. Why is he acting like such a wimp? It's time to remind him of the cautionary tale of Samson and Delilah (especially as he's always been rather proud of his thick head of hair) and at the same time give him a subtle hint about how wet he's being. Send him a **pair of haircutting scissors** with a card reading **"Remember what happened to Samson!"**

*Send a disloyal friend a **set of knives** to show that you are fully aware that they have been stabbing you in the back.*

shops & suppliers

Conservation

Friends of The Earth
Gift Aid Information
UK Tel: 0171-490 1555
International: Amsterdam
(003120) 622 1369

London Zoo
Adopt an animal scheme
Tel: 0171-586 4443

Wild Fowl and Wetland Trust
Slimbridge
Gloucester Gl2 7BT
Tel: 01453-890333
Bird adoption office ext. 262
Sponsor a duck
International enquiries
welcome

World Wide Fund For
Nature
Information UK
Tel: 01483-426 444

Film, Audio & Video

Sureway Ventures
2 Vivien Road,Bradford,
West Yorkshire BD8 0PH
Tel/Fax: 01274-548838
Cine film converted to video, video copying, editing and filming services, slides transferred to photograph or onto video (any format). UK and worldwide service

Flowers

Interflora
Freephone: 0500-434343

Food & Wine

Jane Asher Party Cakes
24 Cale Street
London SW3 3QU
Tel: 0171 584 6177
Cakes made to order in most shapes and sizes

Kloster International
Unit 19
Manor Farm
Beachampton
Milton Keynes
Bucks MK19 6AT
Tel/Fax: 01908-261170
Personalised printing on wine bottle labels

Moffatt Fishery Ltd
Dumfrieshire DG10 9 QL
Tel: 01683-21240
Smoked salmon by
mail order
UK and worldwide service

The Wine Society
A membership organisation run by wine enthusiasts providing its members with a catalogue of the finest wines and spirits from around the world. For details contact the Member Services Department:
The International Exhibition
Co-operative Wine
Society Ltd,
Gunnels Wood Road,
Stevenage,
Herts SG1 2BG
Tel: 01438-741177
Fax: 01438-741392

3D Wines
Holly Lodge,
High Street,
Swineshead,
Lincolnshire PE20 3LH
Tel: 01205-820745
Rent a row of vines

Gardening

BARB
The British Association Representing Breeders can advise on rose and shrub growers who may be willing to name a rose. For information write to:
BARB
The General Secretary
Portland Street
Kings Lynn
Norfolk PE30 1PB

David Austin Roses
Bowling Green Lane
Albrighton, Wolverhampton
West Midlands WV7 3HB
Te: 01902-373931

The Royal National Rose
Society
Gardens of the Rose
Chiswell Green
St. Albans AL2 3NR
Tel: 01727-850461
Suppliers of *Find That Rose*, a book containing the names and suppliers of all named roses, including special occasion roses for birthdays, anniversaries, weddings, births, boys' and girls' names, £2.20 plus p&p.

Health & Beauty

Aromatherapy Associates
68 Maltings Place
Bagleys Lane
London SW6 2BY
Tel: 0171-371 9878
Aromatherapy blends for home care; bath oils, facial oils and body oils
Mail order UK and worldwide

The International
Federation of
Aromatherapists
Stamford House
2-4 Chiswick High Road
London W4 1TH
Tel: 0181-742 2605
Fax: 0181-742 2606
For a directory of registered IFA aromatherapists send £2.00 and an A5 SAE.
Gift vouchers also available.

Jewellery & Silver

Asprey
165-169 New Bond Street
London W1Y OAR
Tel: 0171-493 6767
Fax: 0171-491 0384
Silver, crystal, photograph albums and frames, first and limited edition books, wedding list service, design, engraving and stamping.

Chamberlain Clarke Ltd.
Reco House
928 High Road
North Finchley
London N12 9RW
Tel: 0181-446 9319
Fax: 0181-446 9719
Deskware, penknives, silver cufflinks, accessories and christening presents. Stock items and made to order.
Mail order UK and worldwide

Theo Fennell
177 Fulham Road
London SW3 6JW
Tel: 0171-376 4855

Tiffany & Co.
Jewellery, stationery, international wedding list service, christening gifts, glass and silver items, engraving service available. Branches worldwide include:
25 Old Bond Street
London W1X 3AA
Tel: 0171-409 2790
Fax: 0171-491 3110

The Chifley Plaza
2 Chifley Square
NSW 2000, Aus.
Tel: 61-2-235-1777

Fifth Avenue & 57th Street
New York 10022
Tel: 212-755 8000

85 Bloor Street West, Toronto
Tel: 416-921 3900

Miscellaneous

DHL
24 hour parcel service.
For information: UK Tel:
0345-100 300
Divisions worldwide

International Star Registry
24 Highbury Grove
London N5 2DQ
Tel: 0171-226 6886
Name a star

Stationery

Printed Gifts
31a Duke Street
London W1M 5DF
Tel: 0171-935 1593
Monogrammed pencils, playing cards and matches
Mail order service

Rembrandt Games
Rembrandt House
Whippendale Road,
Watford
Herts WD1 7PG
Tel: 01923-220899
Fax: 01923-256066
Jigsaw puzzles made to order (photographs and pictures) in wood or cardboard.
UK and worldwide orders welcome.

Smythson of Bond Street
44 New Bond Street
London W1Y ODE
Tel: 0171-629 8558
Fax: 0171-495 6111
Personalised stationery, games, leather goods and gift items
Mail order service

Stores with special services

Boots the Chemist
Gifts and customer services:
Tel: 0115 9506111
Wide range of beauty products, film, audio and video accessories, albums and gifts

Fortnum & Mason
181 Piccadilly
London W1A 1ER
Tel: 0171-734 8040
Fax: 0171-437 3278
Gifts and luxury hampers available by mail order.

Harrods Ltd
87-135 Brompton Road
Knightsbridge
London SW1X 7XL
Food orders,
engraving,
monogramming and customer enquires
Tel: 0171-730 1234
Travel Bureau:
Tel: 0171-581 0927
Ticket bookings:
Tel: 0171-589 1101
Executive Shopping Service:
Tel: 0171-581 4874
Gift and Bridal Registry:
Tel: 0171-730 4581
Corporate Gifts:
Tel: 0171-225 5994
Delivery anywhere in the world.

John Lewis Partnership
Peter Jones:
Tel: 0171-730 0200
John Lewis:
Tel: 0171-499 1977
Household and bridal.
Wedding lists

Travel

Eurotunnel
Bookings and information:
UK Tel: 0990-353535

Hilton International
Hotel reservations
Worldwide: 0345-581595

Vintage Newspapers

Historic Newspapers
PO Box 3
Newton Stewart
Wigtownshire
DG8 6TQ
Free phone:
0800 906 609

Yesterday's News
43 Dundonald Road
Colwyn Bay
Clwyd LL29 7RE
Tel: 01492-531195/531303

Weddings

The Wedding List Company
91 Walton Street
London SW3 2HP
Tel: 0171-584 1222
UK and worldwide

acknowledgements

THE PUBLISHER *would like to thank the following people and organizations for the loan of items and services for photography:*

Bennett & Thorogood,
Unit C10,
Grays Mews Antique Market,
Davies Street,
London W1Y 1AR

British Rubber Stamp Co,
10-16 Scrutton St,
London EC2A 4RJ

David Wainwright,
251 Portobello Road,
London W11

C. Farlow & Co,
5 Pall Mall,
London SW1Y 5NP

Force 4 Chandelry,
30 Bressenden Place,
Buckingham Palace Road,
London SW1E 5DG

Fortnum & Mason Ltd,
181 Piccadilly,
London W1A 1ER

Fuji UK Ltd,
1256 Finchley Road,
London NW3 6JH

Graham & Green,
Elgin Crescent,
London Wll 2JA

Greenery Ltd,
Bridge Farm,
Hospital Bridge Road,
Twickenham TW2 6LH

Harrods Ltd,
87-135 Brompton Road,
Knightsbridge,
London SW1X 7XL

Jane Asher Party Cakes,
24 Cale Street,
London SW3 3QU

Mallard Models,
133 Dorset Road,
London SW19

Miele Co Ltd,
Fairacres,
Marcham Road,
Abingdon,
Oxon OX14 1TW

Mulberry Co Ltd,
11-12 Gees Court,
London W1M 5HQ

Nu-line Builders Merchants,
315 Westbourne Park Road,
London W11

Paul's Aquatic World,
Kilburn Square,
London NW6

Telesonic Marine Ltd,
60-64 Brunswick Centre,
London WC1N 1AE